A MEASURE OF KNOWLEDGE

A Measure of Knowledge

JAMES R. SIMMS

PHILOSOPHICAL LIBRARY

New York

Published 1971 by Philosophical Library, Inc.,
15 East 40 Street, New York, New York 10016.

Copyright 1968 by James R. Simms.
Library of Congress Catalog Card No. 71-1181312
SBN 8022-2347-8

Manufactured in the United States of America

To

The Memory of

My Beloved Wife

Polly

TABLE OF CONTENTS

CHAPTER IV — MEASUREMENT OF KNOWLEDGE

CHAPTER V — MINERAL KNOWLEDGE

CHAPTER VI — PLANT KNOWLEDGE

PREFACE

Man has been contemplating the meaning of knowledge at least as long as history has been recorded. A great deal of information has been developed about the learning processes and about knowledge. However, to date there has not been an adequate theory which allows knowledge to be measured and quantified.

A theory of knowledge is presented in this book which provides a basis for measuring and quantifying knowledge. This theory can be essentially summarized as;

> An individual's knowledge is directly proportional to its capacity to direct energy.

The theory is developed from fundamental definitions, axioms and general concepts. Equations are developed relating knowledge to directed energy, units of knowledge are developed, and examples are given for major classes of substances.

The social sciences are considered by many people to be less than a science as they do not have the same degree of rigor as the physical sciences. It is my belief that a measure of knowledge can provide a basis for making the social sciences more rigorous. It is hoped that the theory of knowledge presented in this book can provide a step on the path toward quantification of social phenomena and can provide a rigorous foundation for the social sciences.

A theory of knowledge crosses all branches of science. The early investigations of knowledge were in the realm of philosophy. The psychologist made significant advances in the areas of learning processes and knowledge. The fields of biology, biochemistry, and biophysics are also involved in the search for an understanding of knowledge. A basic theory of knowledge is important to all scientific endeavor.

The theory of knowledge presented herein utilizes the disciplines of mathematics, physics, chemistry, biology, and physiology. The multi-discipline nature of the theory of knowledge requires the presentation of the theory on a very basic level. Background, in a given discipline, is presented as it influences the development of the theory.

The development of knowledge theory presented in this book can be followed with an understanding of elementary calculus. General concepts of the theory can be understood without elementary calculus by reading only the general presentation and the examples. The reader who is interested only in the general theory may omit the paragraphs marked with an asterisk wihout loss of continuity in the development of the theory.

Apologies are given to the specialist as the wide coverage and multi-discipline nature of the theory does not allow a detailed treatment of his particular technology. Only that detail required to develop and present the theory of knowledge has been included. I feel that additional detail would detract from the central theme of the theory.

Apologies are given for the lack of rigor in those areas which are not central to the theory of knowledge. Development of the basic theory is considered to be rigorous, however the calculations given in the examples are intended only to show application of knowledge theory to certain substances and are not precise; nor do they have to be to illustrate basic principles.

The theory of knowledge presented herein allows a quantitative comparison of the knowledge of all things in our universe. The knowledge of a particular individual of a species can be measured for a given environment and can be predicted for other environmental conditions.

I am deeply indebted to Lewey O. Gilstrap Jr., Raymond E. Hoop, and Ram K. Khatri for their valuable comments and constructive criticism during the preparation of this book. I wish to acknowledge my indebtedness to Promila Bagai for assisting in the typing of the book.

A MEASURE OF KNOWLEDGE

Chapter I

INTRODUCTION

1.0 *Historical Investigation of Knowledge*

Knowledge has been the subject of philosophical investigation since the era of the ancient Greeks. Socrates (born about 470 B.C.) probably set the course of Greek thought in the problems of knowledge by accentuating the intimate relation of objective fact to human thought. Introduction of this subjective element into Greek speculation highlighted the problems of knowledge.

Plato (428 B.C.–348 B.C.) continued the investigation of knowledge and presented three theories of the nature of knowledge in the THEAETETUS (completed about 368 B.C.). The three theories presented were: (1) knowledge is identical with sense-apprehension, (2) knowledge is true belief or opinion, and (3) knowledge is true belief accompanied by definition. Plato's intent in the THEAETETUS was to show that these three theories break down under the weight of criticism.

From the early investigations of knowledge by the Greeks, a branch of philosophy has developed which deals with the investigation of the nature and structure of knowledge. This branch of philosophy is called epistemology, the doctrine or theory of knowing. The major question addressed in epistemology is — What is the meaning of to know? This question causes other questions to arise; such as, what is the validity of our knowledge? What sort of things constitute the external world? Do we have definite knowledge or can we only have opinions?

In the latter part of the seventeenth century and during the eighteenth century, a theory of knowledge was developed which is called subjective idealism. The general conclusion of subjective

1

idealism is that the qualities of the world which we preceive by means of our senses are dependent on the mind of the perceiver. The development of this theory was due to the three philosophers Locke, Berkeley, and Hume; sometimes referred to as the empiricists. In essence, the empiricists assert that our knowledge stems from, and is all limited by, sense experience. John Locke (1632–1704) stated in AN ESSAY CONCERNING HUMAN UNDERSTANDING (1690) that his purpose was "to inquire into the original, certainty, and extent of human knowledge, together with the grounds and degrees of belief, opinion, and assent". Locke's conclusions can be stated generally that the mind thinks about its own ideas where idea means "whatever is the object of the understanding, when a man thinks" or "whatever it is which the mind can be employed in thinking".

George Berkeley (1685–1753) extended the theories of Locke in his works A TREATISE CONCERNING THE PRINCIPLES OF HUMAN KNOWLEDGE (1710), and THREE DIA-LOGUES BETWEEN HYLAS AND PHILONOUS IN OPPO-SITION TO SCEPTICS AND ATHEISTS (1713). The empiricists school was essentially killed by the works of David Hume (1771–1776); AN ENQUIRY CONCERNING HUMAN UNDERSTANDING (1748), and DIALOGUES CONCERN-ING NATURAL RELIGION (1779). The empiricists, who claimed that all knowledge derives from experience, through the senses, had shown that if this is really true we not only lose the physical world, the law of cause and effect, and other people, but also ourselves.

Theories of knowledge based on reason were developed in the seventeenth century. Descartes (1596–1650), Leibnitz (1646–1716), and Spinoza (1632–1677) represent the rationalist philosophers who relied upon the operation of the reasoning faculty to give them knowledge about the universe. The ratio-nalist theory resulted in an internally consistent system which was isolated from real fact.

Many theories of knowledge have been developed since the empiricists and the rationalists. These include the theories, or systems, of such great philosophers as Immanuel Kant (1724–

1804), Hegel (1770–1831), G. E. Moore, and Bertrand Russell, to mention a few. Most philosophers seem to agree with the Kantian view that things in the physical world behave in accordance with the requirements of the a priori reason because they are to a large extent the product of that reason. Stated more precisely, even if they themselves exist in their own right, the laws governing their behavior are those which our mind has prescribed to them. According to this viewpoint, the laws of things and the laws of thought are the same, for the sufficient reason that the characteristics of things are the products of thought.

Needless to say, there is not presently a theory of knowledge that is completely acceptable to contemporary philosophers. Indeed there may never be a completely deterministic solution to the problems of epistemology. Niels Bohr has suggested that the problems of epistemology are similar to the problems of a causal description in atomic physics in that the phenomenon being observed cannot be isolated from observing devices (Reference 1.1). Heisenberg recognized the observational problem in atomic physics and developed an uncertainty principle to describe the problem. The key point of this principle being that a precise causal relation cannot be found for atomic processes of quantum action, in the normal classical physics sense, due to the unavoidable interaction between the atomic objects being observed and the measuring instruments necessary for these observations. Any investigation in epistemological problems is bound to suffer from the observed-observer problem.

1.1 *Knowledge-Personal or General*

The epistemological branch of philosophy treats the theories of *our* knowledge. The questions of epistemology are related to *man's* knowledge; what *we* know; the validity of *our* knowledge. Knowledge is treated as a personal possession of man in the epistemological theories of knowledge.

I believe that knowledge should apply universally to all things. It is difficult for me to conceive of man being the only "knowing" organism in the universe. For example, experiments have been performed where a monkey was given two sticks which could be fitted together to make a longer stick and food was placed at a distance outside the cage so that it was unobtainable with one stick. The monkey, after trying unsuccessfully with one stick, joined the two sticks and obtained the food. Obviously the monkey not only knows about his environment but has sufficient knowledge to successfully reason about the environment. All animals, to some extent, know about their outside world sufficiently well for them to exist; to me, this represents knowledge. Indeed, there exist in the literature many arguments for there being intelligent machines. References 1.2 thru 1.5 are recent publications in which arguments are presented concerning machine intelligence. If other things can know and have knowledge, then what is an objective meaning of knowledge? and is there commonality or unity of knowledge for all things?

It is my intent to present a theory of knowledge which is not restricted to *our* knowledge. It is very important for the understanding of the theory of knowledge presented in this book to keep clearly in mind the difference between knowledge and *our* knowledge. Throughout the book I use knowledge in a general sense and not as *our* knowledge.

1.2 *Measurement of Knowledge*

A useful theory of knowledge is one that allows the theory to be verified and allows knowledge to be measured and quantified. I believe that Lord Kelvin stated the need for measurement very well in the following quote: "I often say that when you can measure what you are speaking about, and express it in numbers, you know something about it; but when you cannot measure it, when you cannot express it in numbers, your knowledge is of a meagre and unsatisfactory kind; it may be the beginning of knowledge, but you have scarcely, in your thoughts, advanced to the stage of Science, whatever the matter may be."

If a theory of knowledge can be developed which will allow knowledge to be measured, we will have taken the first small

4

step along the path of a science of knowledge. It is my intent to present a theory of knowledge which is conducive to the measurement of knowledge. Again, it should be kept in mind that I am talking about general knowledge and not *our* knowledge.

One would hope that the theories of epistemology would furnish a background for a theory of knowledge that would be general and that would allow a measure of knowledge. Unfortunately, the theories of knowledge resulting from epistemological studies are not conducive to extensions or extrapolations which allow measurement of knowledge.

1.3 *A General Theory of Knowledge*

The problem before us is the development of a theory for a measure of general knowledge. To be truly general, the theory must be applicable to all things, animate and inanimate. The knowledge of animals, plants and minerals should be subject to quantification. We should be able to answer such questions as, how much knowledge does a given animal species have? What is the knowledge of a man of a given culture and how does it compare to that of man in another culture? Do plants have knowledge? If so, how much? Do minerals have knowledge? If so, how much and how does it compare to that of man and other animals? Do computers and adaptive learning machines have knowledge?

An adequate theory of knowledge should allow the above listed questions to be answered. At the present time, answers to these questions are in the realm of opinions as there is not a method for making a determination. Indeed the arguments and opinions seem to depend on the strength of feeling one has for knowledge being reserved only for man. The theory I present in this book will allow the above listed questions concerning knowledge to be answered.

The general theory of knowledge presented herein is based on a slightly more precise and more operationally oriented definition of knowledge than the common usage definition. It is normal to establish a more precise definition of a term to be used in mathematical or scientific investigation than the common use definition. The definition of probability is a case in point; however, almost any scientific term could be used as an example. The definition of knowledge to be used in the theory is obtained by asking – why does anything have knowledge? or why does anything know? These questions are different from the normal epistemological questions, i.e. what is the nature of knowledge and what are the limitations of our knowledge? Let us assume for a moment that a man does have the capacity to know; then, let us ask the question – why does he know? In asking why he knows, we must ask, when did he first begin to know? For instance, did he begin to know when he developed symbols and could think in abstract terms or did he know when he first evolved on this earth? It is obvious that primitive man could distinguish one thing from another, could perceive directly and could discern the character of things; therefore he had the capability to know. I doubt that there can be disagreement that primitive man had the capability to know and hence had some knowledge. The question remains – why does he know? There is a preponderance of evidence to indicate that the senses, which allow man and other animals to obtain information regarding the outside world, develop in response to the local environment. For instance, animals living in absolute darkness do not develop eyes, man living in absolute darkness suffers atrophy of the eyes and hence loses his ability to sense light. Indeed, all animals adapt to their local environment. It can be stated, with great confidence, that man and other animals know so they can fit into their environment. If the environment changes to such an extent that the environmental energy which activates an animal's sensor becomes extinct, then after a period of adaptation, which may take many generations, the sensor disappears and the animal can no longer know about those things which can only be perceived by that sense. We can conclude that man knows and has knowledge so he can adjust to, cope with, and fit into his environment.

To fit into the environment, man must be able to receive energy from the environment and must be able to release energy into the environment. That is, he must be capable of directing an energy exchange with the environment. The adaptations of animals which allow them to know about their environment are related to their ability to survive in the environment, where survival in the environment requires the direction of energy.

I now define knowledge as the ability of a substance to direct energy. This definition of knowledge, which is based on why something has knowledge, provides a utilitarian or operational definition which encompasses the majority of the common usage definitions of knowledge. The theory of knowledge presented herein is based on this more precise definition of knowledge. The definition is further developed in Chapter II.

The general theory of knowledge developed in this book results in the following summary statement;

An individual's knowledge is directly proportional to its capacity to direct energy.

It will be shown that the individual can be anything; animate or inanimate. In addition, it will be shown that the proportionality constant can be determined and that the directed energy can be measured and/or determined. Hence, it will be shown that we have a theory that is both general and which can provide quantitative values for knowledge. This concept of knowledge can be utilized to explain many of the phenomena in nature, and as a general theory that relates knowledge and energy for all substances in the universe.

1.4 Scope and Organization of the Book

The book is organized to proceed from a general background introductory discussion to the development of the mathematical equations relating knowledge and energy, to values of knowledge for representative individual substances.

In Chapter II, fundamental definitions are presented and a basic axiom is developed. Heuristic arguments are presented to show the validity of the axiom to our everyday concept of knowledge. Additional axioms are presented which establish limiting conditions for knowledge. The axioms presented in

Chapter II form the basic foundation of the general knowledge theory presented in this book.

The basic equations relating knowledge to energy are developed in Chapted III. These equations are used along with the concept of survival energy of a substance to relate knowledge to the environment. Fundamental properties of knowledge are derived from the equations and the relationships between knowledge and information are discussed.

In Chapter IV, the measurement of knowledge is discussed. The units for knowledge are presented and a system of units selected. The arguments for and against the various measurements of knowledge are presented and the selection of a particular method is presented.

The theory of knowledge, as it applies to minerals, is given in Chapter V. The general characteristics of minerals are reviewed and the characteristics essential for the application of the theory of knowledge to minerals are identified. The energy relations for minerals and their environment, and for the energy directed by the mineral are developed. Expressions for the knowledge of minerals are developed based on these energy relationships. An example is given to demonstrate the method for calculating the knowledge of hydrogen.

A theory of knowledge for plants is presented in Chapter VI. A definition of a living organism is given and the general characteristics of plants are discussed. The characteristics of plants that are essential to the theory of knowledge are identified. The equations which relate plant knowledge to energy are developed. These equations allow the determination of the energy directed by a plant and the knowledge of the plant. The information relations for plants are discussed and is related to plant knowledge. Two examples of plant knowledge are presented to illustrate the application of the knowledge theory to plants. The plants chosen as examples are bacteria, which is the smallest living organism, and the Giant Sequoia, which is the largest living organism.

The theory of knowledge is extended to animals in Chapter VII. The general characteristics of animals are reviewed and those essential to the development of knowledge theory and measurement are identified. The knowledge-energy relations for animals are developed and represented in equation form. The directed energy for animals includes both internal energy and the energy in the environment that is directed by the animal. An example is given which indicates the application of knowledge theory to man.

Chapter VIII gives a summary of the theory of knowledge as it applies to all things. The intent of the summary is to state the essence of knowledge theory, place the theory in perspective, and indicate the utility of the theory.

Chapter II

FUNDAMENTAL CONCEPTS

2.0 *Fundamental Notions*

The fundamental notions presented herein are based on precise definitions of 1) energy, 2) the environment, 3) a substance, 4) survival, and 5) knowledge. The concept of knowledge and the formulation of the knowledge-energy relation are developed from these terms, which are defined as follows:

Energy: The capacity for doing work. As used herein, energy has the properties and attributes defined in the science of physics.

Environment: The sum of the energy surrounding a given body or substance, i.e., all the energy in an energy system that is not located in the substance. The environmental energy may act or tend to act on the substance; however, this is not a necessary condition.

Substance: A substance is anything that has fundamental or characteristic qualities. More specifically, anything that has fundamental or characteristic physical and/or chemical properties. We will be dealing with the measurable properties and characteristics which allow the identification of a substance and the discrimination of one substance from other substances.

Survival: Remaining in existence and/or continued existence. As used herein, survival denotes the continued existence of a substance where existence of the substance is defined by the retention of fundamental characteristics and properties of the substance.

Knowledge: The fundamentals of the knowledge theory must be based on a precise definition of knowledge. A rather loose definition of knowledge was given in Chapter I; it is necessary

11

to provide a more solid foundation for the definition of knowledge. Let us start with the common usage definitions of knowledge. These are: a clear and certain perception of that which exists, or of truth and fact; learning; skill; acquaintance with any fact or person; cognizance, recognition; information, power of knowing. From this point of departure, we ask not the epistemological questions-what is the meaning of knowledge? and what are the limits or our knowledge? but why do substances have knowledge? that is, why do substances perceive that which exists? why do substances have fact? From the arguments presented in Chapter I, these questions were answered by the statement — substances have knowledge so they can adjust to, cope with, and fit into the environment. Stated slightly differently, knowledge is the perception of that which exists in the environment, and especially is the perception of that fact required for adjustment to the environment. It should be noted that the last definition does not contain we, nor is it intended to be restricted to man.

Let us now examine what is meant by the statement: to adjust to, cope with, and fit into the environment. All adjustments to the environment must be made by some form of energy adjustment. In Chapter I, we examined the deletion of light energy from the environment; i.e., electromagnetic energy in the visible spectrum. The adjustment made by animals to this situation is that light energy can no longer be utilized or directed by the animal. In general, an adjustment to the environment requires a substance to direct energy in some way. There are many examples to illustrate this point, a few are as follows. If the solar energy level increases to a high level, an animal must perceive this fact and take action to avoid high energy levels which would cause the animal to die. If the thermal energy of the environment decreases to a below normal level for a given animal, then the animal must either direct additional energy in the environment, move to another local environment, or die. In the examples given, it was required that a substance direct energy in order to adapt to the environment; the alternative is not to adapt and, hence, not survive.

Let us now question the statement — a clear and certain

perception of that which exists. A more fundamental statement is: a clear and certain determination of the states of the environment and of the substance. As all substances are made up of energy (matter is energy), the most basic statement is; a clear and certain determination of the energy states of the substance and the environment. Reduction of the common usage definition of knowledge to the basic fundamentals of nature, as in the above heuristic discussion, results in the following definition of knowledge: the determination of the energy states of the substance and its environment for the purpose of directing energy which will allow the substance to adjust to, cope with, and fit into its environment. As it is understood that the knowledge being described is of a particular substance, the definition can be shortened to: *knowledge is the capacity to direct energy*. This definition of knowledge is based on a more fundamental consideration of the common usage definition of knowledge; therefore, the common usage definitions can be derived from our basic definition.

2.1 *Basic Knowledge-Energy Relationship*

We are not, at this stage, at liberty to make a statement about the way energy is directed by a substance. We can, based on our definition of knowledge, make the statement that knowledge is related to directed energy. The amount of knowledge should be related to the amount of directed energy in some way. That is, if a substance (A) has the capacity to direct more energy than another substance (B), then the first substance (A) should have more knowledge than substance (B). The only definite statement we are at liberty to make is that the amount of knowledge is a function of the amount of energy the substance is capable of directing. If we let k be the amount of knowledge of a substance and e_d be the amount of energy the substance can direct, then we can state;

AXIOM I

$$k = F(e_d) \qquad (2.1)$$

where $F(e_d)$ represents a function of e_d. That is, the amount of knowledge of a substance is a function of the energy the substance can direct. It should be noted that a substance does not necessarily will that energy be directed.

2.2 Heuristic Arguments

To illustrate the applicability of the axiom to our background and experience, let us consider the relationships among the environment, knowledge, and survival of a human. It is obvious that a man must have sufficient knowledge to extract the amount of food from the environment that will keep him alive. It is equally well understood that a man must have sufficient knowledge to protect himself from extremes in the environment such as cold and heat, if he is to survive. The first statement above can be reworded as follows. Man must have sufficient knowledge to obtain energy from the environment to satisfy his minimum energy requirements if he is to survive. The second statement above can be reworded as follows. Man must have sufficient knowledge to alter his contiguous environment if he is to survive in an extreme energy environment.

Additional illustrations of the applicability of axiom I are obtained by examining a variety of cases which are recognized as major discoveries by man, i.e., increases in knowledge, such as 1) fire, 2) the ability to domesticate animals, 3) the ability to grow foodstuffs, 4) explosives (gun powder), 5) printing, 6) the major laws of the physical sciences, and 7) atomic energy. These are but a few of the major discoveries, however they are sufficient to illustrate the point. Let us now consider each in turn to see if a basic relationship exists between knowledge and directed energy for these cases.

Fire: The discovery of fire enabled man to obtain a measure of control over the local thermal energy environment. Fire gave man the ability to control his contiguous or local energy environment (thermal) so that he could now exist and survive in a more extreme environment than before, i.e., man had learned to direct a limited amount of thermal energy.

Domestic Animals: Domestication of beasts of burden allowed

14

man to expend less of his energy to perform a given chore and to perform chores that were previously beyond his energy capacity. In this case, through the use of knowledge, man had more available energy. That is, man had learned to direct the activities of animals to obtain more useful energy for his own use.

Growing Foodstuffs: When man discovered how to cultivate plants to obtain food, he was able to either (1) obtain his minimum food requirements (energy) for less energy expended in search of food, or (2) he was able to expend the same amount of his energy and survive in an environment that normally would not provide his minimum survival energy. In this case he is directing some of the energy of the environment.

Explosives: The invention of explosives gave man the ability to direct high energies to change his local environment.

Printing: The invention of the printing press affects the knowledge-energy relationship in a number of ways. The knowledge of printing allows more information to be presented for less expenditure of man's energy, i.e., man's hand written script. In the absence of recorded information, additional energy must be expended by each generation in the redevelopment or rediscovery of information.

Major Laws of Physical Science: The major laws of the physical sciences such as Newton's laws of mechanics, and Maxwell's equations of electromagnetic fields, permit man to utilize the energy of the environment for his own purposes or to control the energy of the environment by reducing the amount of energy required to be expended by man in order to survive. In this case, man had learned better ways to direct the energy in the physical environment.

Atomic Energy: The discovery of atomic energy gave man a vast new source of directed energy that can be used to change the ambient energy environment, i.e., utilized to add or subtract heat energy, electromagnetic energy, etc. The know-

15

ledge of atomic energy is a graphic example of the relationship between knowledge and directed energy.

Although only a few examples have given to show the relation between knowledge and energy for man, the concept is readily extended to cover a vast range of knowledge.

The concept of knowledge applies to all animals as they must direct energy to survive. That is, all animals have a required minimum energy intake that allows survival and they must have sufficient knowledge to extract this energy from the environment. Animals have knowledge which allows them to change their ambient environment as witnessed by their ability to build shelters (dens, lairs, nest, burrows, etc.). In addition, certain animals have sufficient knowledge which allows them to contend with a changing energy environment. Examples of this are the hibernating species, changing in surface susceptibility to energy changes, such as growing layers of fat, and growing longer and thicker hair. The well known facts about animals stated above demonstrate that the knowledge-energy relation is applicable to animals. As far as I can determine, there are no exceptions to the general knowledge-energy relation in the animal world.

The knowledge relationship also applies to plant life. Plants have knowledge which allows them to extract, i.e., direct, sufficient energy from the environment for survival. The processes whereby a plant transforms energy into a form that can be utilized by the plant are well known and are treated in most text books on botany and biology. Obviously, the plants that exist today and survive from generation to generation have developed sufficient knowledge to allow them to deal with the changing environmental energy conditions. Casual observation of the plants around us shows us that they change their surface conditions (loss of leaves in the fall, growth of new leaves in spring) to allow for the changes in environmental energy conditions.

The interaction between nonliving substances and the energy environment can be considered in the same frame of reference as living things. Consider a substance that has well defined physical and chemical properties. To survive in a given state

16

and maintain the same physical and chemical properties, it must accept a given amount of energy from the environment. As an example, let us consider water. To remain in the liquid state, i.e., not freeze, water must absorb a given amount of energy as a function of time. Other liquids exhibit the same properties, the difference being the amount of energy required from the environment, the organization of the substance, the utilization of the energy, and the flow of energy back into the environment. Therefore it can be stated, in general, that for nonliving substances to survive, they must direct energy and hence must have sufficient knowledge to obtain energy from the environment to allow their existence in a particular state. There are substances which can exist in the absence of an energy exchange with the environment. Pure energy, such as electromagnetic radiation, can exist with no interaction with the environment. In addition, some materials can exist as mass with no energy input, i.e., at zero degrees absolute temperature. It will be shown in later chapters that these substances also have directed energy and hence knowledge.

The interaction between minerals and the energy of the environment have been the subject of many studies. The properties of these interactions for many minerals are well known. For our purposes, we will give the attribute of knowledge to the mineral's capability of interacting with the energy of the environment. This capability is usually in the form of either absorbing the energy from the environment, repelling (reflecting) the energy from the environment, or radiating energy into the environment.

2.3 *Knowledge Limits*

The epistemologist searches for an answer to the question — what is the limit of *our* knowledge? We are interested in the question — what are the limits of a substance's knowledge? We would like to know both the lower and the upper limit of a substance's knowledge. Let us first investigate the lower limit of knowledge. Intuitively one feels that the lower limit should be zero, i.e., negative knowledge should be precluded. Consideration of the definition of knowledge proves our intuition to be correct. Absolute energy, as defined in the physical sciences, is nonnegative; that is, energy can have values of zero or greater but it can never be less than zero. Therefore the energy directed by a substance must be equal to or greater than zero. If a substance does not have the capacity to direct energy, then it is not knowledgeable. The common usage definition of knowledge does not allow a concept of negative knowledge. As far as I have been able to determine, a concept of negative knowledge has never been considered in either common usage or in the scientific literature. Based on these considerations, I postulate the following;

AXIOM II

The knowledge of a substance is equal to or greater than zero, i.e.,

$$k \geq 0.$$

Our intuition does not provide clear answers to the question of the upper limit of knowledge. The word omniscient implies one having universal knowledge or being infinitely wise. Man seems to allow the concept of an unbounded or infinite knowledge. Using the definition of knowledge presented herein, the upper limit of knowledge is associated with the direction, by a substance, of all available energy. If we were to consider the complete universe, then the absolute knowledge would be related to the direction by a substance of all the energy in the universe. If we were to use some reference system other that the complete universe, then the upper limit of knowledge, referenced to this system, is associated with the direction, by the substance, of all the energy in this new reference system. I postulate that a viable concept of an upper limit of knowledge can be related to the total energy in a defined system of energy and the energy in that system which is directed by the substance under consideration. This concept will allow the consideration of absolute knowledge, which is related to the total energy in the universe, and the relative knowledge with respect to some defined energy system. The defined energy

18

system can be a local environment or any other defined system, as long as it is identified and specified.

The upper limit of knowledge in the above postulated concept is related to the direction, by the substance, of all the energy in the system. It is sometime convenient to normalize the directed energy by dividing the directed energy by the total energy in the system. By this normalization process, the upper limit of knowledge for all defined energy systems is a function of the ratio of the directed energy to the total available energy in the system. As it is obvious that the directed energy can never exceed the available energy of the system, we can state the following;

AXIOM III

The upper limit of knowledge is a function of the ratio of the directed energy to the total available energy (e_t);

$$ k = F \left(\frac{e_d}{e_t} \right) $$

where the ratio $\left(\dfrac{e_d}{e_t} \right)$ is equal to or less than one;

i.e.,

$$ \left(\frac{e_d}{e_t} \right) \leq 1. $$

2.4 Summary

Precise definitions were developed for the fundamental elements on which the general theory of knowledge will be based. The fundamental axiom relating knowledge and directed energy was developed from these definitions. Heuristic arguments were given to show that knowledge, as commonly used, can readily be shown to be related to directed energy. The heuristic arguments were then extended to show that all substances have knowledge. It was argued that all living substances are transformers of energy, i.e. utilizers and directors of energy, and hence must have knowledge which allows the utilization of energy. Inanimate objects are also transformers of energy in the sense that they absorb energy in one form or frequency range and release energy in another form or frequency range.

Axioms were presented which establish the upper and lower limits of the amount of energy which can be directed and hence can be used to establish the upper and lower limits of knowledge. The fundamental axiom (I) and the two limit axioms will be used in the following chapters to develop the equations relating knowledge and energy.

CHAPTER III

MATHEMATICAL FORMULATION

3.0 *Introduction*

The definitions, concepts, notions, and axioms presented in Chapter II are used in this chapter to develop a fundamental mathematical equation for knowledge. This fundamental equation relates knowledge to the energy that a substance directs and the total energy in a given energy system. The total energy is shown to be made up of mutually exclusive energy in the substance and in the environment. The energies in the substance and the environment are shown to be quantities which can be expressed mathematically, and can be predicted and measured. The composition of the directed energy is shown and expressions for directed energies are developed.

The general characteristics of substances which are important to the theory of knowledge are presented. In particular, the characteristics of the basic physical elements are presented as they relate to knowledge. The conditions for survival of a substance are discussed and the characteristics of the more sophisticated substances are considered. The chapter is concluded with a discussion of the relationship between information and knowledge.

3.1 *Fundamental Equations of Knowledge*

The fundamental relationship between knowledge and directed energy was developed in Chapter II in functional form and was stated as axiom I. To be useful in the measurement and prediction of knowledge, the exact form of the functional relation must be developed. Let us start this development by investigating some of the general properties of the function $F(e_d)$. We know that the directed energy must always be greater than or equal to zero, i.e., $e_d \geq 0$, as it is self-evident that the concept of energy does not permit negative energy. Therefore, all energy must be greater than zero and as the directed energy is a subset of all energy, it must be greater than zero. Axiom II states that knowledge must be greater than or equal to zero, therefore if we map the function $F(e_d)$ into a rectangular coordinate system with the directed energy (e_d) as the abscissa and knowledge as the ordinate, the function $F(e_d)$ must lie in the upper right hand plane of this coordinate system. That is, the function is valid only for positive values of knowledge and directed energy. The region of validity for the function is shown in Figure 3-1 by the shaded area.

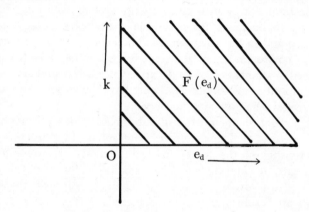

VALID REGION FOR $F(e_d)$

Figure 3-1

An investigation into the form of the function is now in order. It is my belief that for every value of directed energy there can be one and only one value of knowledge. I cannot conceive of a situation where it might be desirable to represent one value of knowledge for two or more values of directed energy. I therefore postulate that the function $F(e_d)$ is single valued, i.e., for each value of directed energy there is a unique value of knowledge. As the directed energy changes value, knowledge will take a corresponding change in value which is uniquely defined by the value for directed energy. Let us assume the convenient sign convention that an increase in directed energy results in an increase in knowledge. That is, for an incremental increase in directed energy there is a corresponding incremental increase in knowledge, i.e., knowledge is a monotonically increasing function of directed energy. Stated less precisely, the more energy a substance can direct, the more knowledge it has or conversely the more knowledge a substance has the more energy it can direct.

It appears to me that a change in directed energy should result in a proportional change in knowledge. I can think of no reason for the ratio of knowledge to directed energy to change as the directed energy varies over its allowable range. Therefore, I postulate that knowledge is directly proportional to the directed energy. Based on this postulate, the function assumes the form of a straight line; that is,

$$k = F(e_d) = Se_d + Y_0 \quad,$$

where S is the slope of the line and Y_0 is the intercept of the line with the ordinate (knowledge axis).

We know that Y_0 cannot be negative as this would result in values of knowledge which are less than zero when the directed energy is zero; axiom II stated that knowledge must be greater than zero. Based on the definitions and concepts developed in Chapter II, knowledge should be zero when the directed energy is zero; i.e., in the absence of directed energy, there cannot be kowledge. Therefore the value of Y_0 must be Zero.

Based on the above stated conditions, the functions $F(e_d)$ must be of the form shown in Figure 3-2. Stated symbolically, we have that $F(e_d)$ must equal Se_d where S is a constant. Therefore

$$k = Se_d \qquad \text{for } e_d \geqq 0 \qquad (3.1)$$

Equation 3.1 is completely general and will apply to any energy system, however in most cases of interest we will be able to define the energy system and hence the total energy in the system.

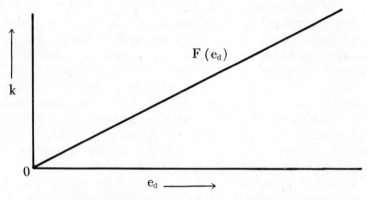

FUNCTIONAL RELATION BETWEEN KNOWLEDGE
AND DIRECTED ENERGY

Figure 3-2

Let us define an energy system with total energy e_t and let us assume that this energy system is sufficiently large so that the total energy can be considered to be constant. We can normalize equation 3.1 with respect to the total energy in the system by setting

$$S = B/e_t$$

where B is a new constant of proportionality. Substituting this value of S into equation 3.1 obtains

$$k = B\,(e_d/e_t).$$

From axiom III, we know that the ratio of the directed energy to the total energy is valid in the range from zero to one. Therefore equation 3.1 becomes;

$$k = B\,(e_d/e_t), \qquad\qquad 0 \le e_d/e_t \le 1 \qquad (3.2)$$

or

$$k = Se_d \qquad\qquad 0 \le e_d \le e_t \qquad (3.3)$$

The proportionality constants S and B could be any positive real number; depending on the units of measure selected. A graph of equation 3.3 is shown in Figure 3-3.

24

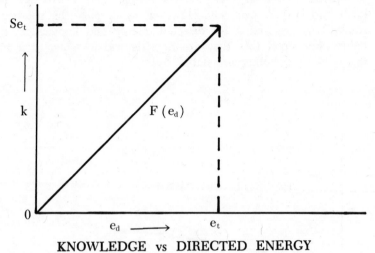

KNOWLEDGE vs DIRECTED ENERGY

Figure 3-3

The function given in equation 3.3 is the fundamental equation of knowledge which will allow a measure of knowledge. It should be noted that specification of the energy system must include at least all the energy directed by the substance.

Development of the fundamental equation of knowledge (equation 3.3) placed very few restrictions on any of the parameters of the equation; i.e., knowledge, directed energy, and total energy. The total energy was considered to be defined and constant for a given energy system and it was implied that the total energy remains constant with time. The directed energy can change with time and hence knowledge can change with time.

In general, one expects directed energy and knowledge to change with time, within given limits. For example, the directed energy and hence knowledge of an animal would be expected to increase after birth, level off at maturity, possibly decrease with advanced age, and become zero at death. Knowledge, as a function of time, might be as shown in Figure 3-4.

As directed energy and knowledge are functions of time, the precise notation for directed energy and knowledge is $e_d(t)$ and $k(t)$ respectively. However, to simplify the notation we will use e_d and k for directed energy and knowledge; it being understood that they are time dependent when used in this book unless otherwise stated.

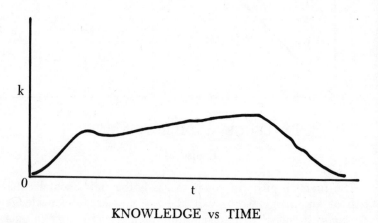

KNOWLEDGE vs TIME

Figure 3-4

Up to this point, the total energy in the energy system has been considered as a single entity. The total energy can be considered as being constituted of two separate and mutually exclusive energies, namely the energy of the substance and the energy of the environment, the energy in the environment being all the remainder of the energy in the system that does not belong to the substance. Consider the energy system shown in Figure 3-5, at any time (t), the total energy (e_t) in the closed system shown in this figure is divided between the mutually exclusive energies of the substance and the environment. That is,

$$e_t = e_s + e_e \qquad (3.4)$$

where:

26

e_s is the energy of the substance at time t,
e_e is the energy of the environment at time t.

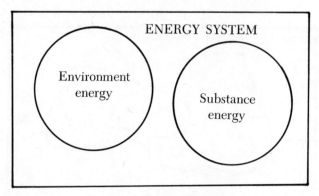

ENERGY SYSTEM

Figure 3-5

There can be a continual exchange of energy between the substance and the environment but the energy must be in one or the other and, by the law of conservation of energy, the sum of the energy in the substance and in the environment must be equal to the total energy in the system. Substitution of equation 3.4 into the fundamental equation for knowledge (3.3), we obtain,

$$k = Se_d \qquad\qquad 0 \leqq e_d \leqq e_s + e_e \qquad (3.5)$$

Equation 3.5 can be stated in words as follows. The total knowledge of a substance is equal to a constant times the energy the substance can direct, where the directed energy can range between zero and the total available energy. The sum of the energy of the substance and the energy of the environment is equal to the total energy in an energy system and therefore represents the total available energy.

The general relationship among the directed energy, environmental energy, the substance energy, and the total energy in any given closed system or universe is shown pictorially in Figure 3-6.

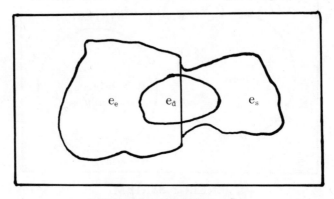

DIRECTED ENERGY SET

Figure 3-6

The directed energy is a subset of the energy in the substance and the energy in the environment. That is, the energy which can be directed by a substance may be within the energy system of the substance or the environment or both. Denoting the energy in the substance which is directed as e_{ds}, that is, the union of the directed energy and the substance energy, and the energy in the environment which is directed as e_{de}; that is, the union of the directed energy and the environment energy, then by the conservation of energy law, we have;

$$e_d = e_{ds} + e_{de} \qquad (3.6)$$

Substituting equation 3.6 into the fundamental knowledge equation (3.3), we obtain;

$$k = S\,(e_{ds} + e_{de}) = Se_{ds} + Se_{de} \qquad (3.7)$$

From our basic definition of knowledge, the term Se_{ds} is the knowledge of the substance related to itself and Se_{de} is the

28

knowledge of the substance related to its environment. Let us designate Se_{ds} and Se_{de} by k_s and k_e respectively. Then we have,

$$k = k_s + k_e \qquad (3.8)$$

The directed substance and the directed environment energies could be divided into any number of energy subsets, say n, then the total directed energy would become;

$$e_d = \sum_{i=0}^{n} e_{di} \qquad (3.9)$$

Hence, the knowledge of the substance becomes

$$k = S \sum_{i=0}^{n} e_{di} \qquad 0 \leqq \sum e_{di} \leqq e_t \qquad (3.10)$$

This knowledge can also be expressed as

$$k = \sum_{i=0}^{n} k_i \qquad (3.11)$$

Where the k_i's are associated with the e_{di}'s. We have just proved an important theorem, namely;

THEOREM I

The total knowledge possessed by a substance, at any given time, is the sum of all the knowledge the substance has about: (1) its own elements, and (2) the elements of the environment.

3.2 *Substance Energy*

To obtain a *measure* of knowledge, it is necessary to quantify the energy relations given in the equations of Paragraph 3.1, that is, we must be able to compute or measure values for

29

substance energy, environment energy, and directed energy. We will first investigate the properties of substance energy.

A substance has been defined in Paragraph 2.0 as anything that has fundamental or characteristic qualities. A substance can be considered as a particular arrangement of mass and energy which has particular fundamental characteristics. All the mass of the substance is actually energy as can be seen by the well known Einstein energy-mass equation ($E = mc^2$), a substance can be considered as energy in a particular form and with particular characteristics.

The total energy of a substance at any given instant of time is equal to the sum of all the energies that make up the substance, i.e., the energies that the substance possesses. These energies can be classified in terms of the energy of the mass that makes up the substance, the thermal energy of the substance, the chemical energy of the substance, mechanical energy of the substance (with respect to the substance and to the environment), etc. Stated in equation form, we have:

$$e_s = e_{sm} + e_{sT} + e_{sc} + e_{sk} + \cdots\cdots\cdots = \sum_j e_{sj} \qquad (3.12)$$

Where:

    e_s is the total energy of the substance
    e_{sm} is the mass energy of the substance (i.e., $e_{sm} = mc^2$)
    e_{sT} is the thermal energy of the substance
    e_{sk} is the mechanical energy of the substance
    e_{sc} is the chemical energy of the substance
    e_{sj} is the energy of the substance in a given form j.

The energies that make up a substance are internal to the substance. These internal energies can be permanent, semipermanent or transient in the substance. The permanent energies can be considered as constituting the basic organization of the substance. The semipermanent energies can be stored in a substance and can be used in the process of energy exchange with the environment. The transient energies in the substance are those which are being exchanged with the environment.

The organizational energies are shown later to be greater than the semipermanent and the transient energies. If we let e_0 be the organizational energy, e_x be the semipermanent energy and e_y be the transient energy of a substance, then we have the following expression for the internal energy of a substance;

$$e_s = e_0 + e_x + e_y \qquad (3.13)$$

The internal energy can be in the form of mass, thermal, radiant, chemical, and mechanical energy.

3.3 *Environment Energy*

The environment of a substance has been previously defined as the sum of the energy surrounding the substance, i.e., all the energy in an energy system that is not in the substance. This includes all the energy that can act on the substance or can be acted upon by the substance. The environment energy in any energy system such as shown in Figure 3-5 includes (1) the energies of all the other substances located within the energy system, and (2) the free energies in the energy system, such as radiant energy.

The total energy in the environment at any given instant of time for an energy system is:

$$e_e = \sum_s \epsilon_s + \sum_{ez} \qquad (3.14)$$

Where,

ϵ_s is the energy of the other substances in the environment ment

e_{ez} is the radiant energy in the environment

Equation 3.14 states that the total energy in the environment at any given instant of time is equal to the sum of the total energy of all the substances that make up the environment plus the sum of all the radiant energy in the environment.

3.4 *Substance-Environment Energy Exchange*

The expressions for the energy of a substance and the energy in the environment, as given in Paragraphs 3.2 and 3.3 respec-

31

tively, are for any given point in time. As time changes, the energies in the substance and the environment varies due to the flow of energy between the substance and the environment. A closed system showing the flow of energy between the environment and the substance is shown in Figure 3-7.

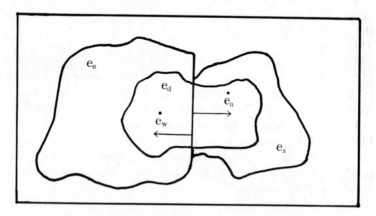

SUBSTANCE-ENVIRONMENT ENERGY FLOW

Figure 3-7

Let us denote the flow of energy from the environment to the substance by $\dot{e}_a$ and the flow of energy from the substance by $\dot{e}_w$, where;

$\dot{e}_a = \dfrac{de_a}{dt}$ is the rate of flow of energy from the environment that is accepted by the substance.

$\dot{e}_w = \dfrac{de_w}{dt}$ is the rate of flow of energy from the substance that is accepted by the environment.

The energy accepted by a substance, e_a, can be in the form

32

of mass (e_m), mechanical (e_k), thermal (e_T), chemical (e_c), radiant (e_z) energy, etc. The equation for accepted energy is:

$$e_a = e_m + e_k + e_T + e_c + e_z + \cdots\cdots\cdots \tag{3.15}$$

The energy accepted by a substance can be related to the energy which flows from the substance to the environment and the energy of the substance. Based on the law of energy conservation, i.e., energy is neither created nor destroyed, the energy accepted by a substance must either cause an increase in the substance's energy or it must be released by the substance to the environment. That is, the accepted energy is equal to the energy released to the environment (e_w) plus the change in the substance's energy (Δe_s). The relationship among accepted, released, and substance energy is:

$$e_a = e_w + \Delta e_s \tag{3.16}$$

or

$$e_a - e_w = \Delta e_s.$$

The relationship among the accepted, released, and substance energy can be expressed in terms of flow rates as follows:

$$\dot{e}_a - \dot{e}_w = \dot{e}_s. \tag{3.17}$$

The energy released from the substance to the environment can be in the form of mass (e_m), mechanical (e_k), thermal (e_T), chemical (e_c), radiant (e_z) energy, etc. Therefore the released energy (e_w) can be in the same form as the accepted energy.

At a given time (t), the energy in the environment is;

$$e_e = e_{e0} + \Delta e_e \tag{3.18}$$

where;

Δe_e is the change in the environment energy during the time interval between t_0 and t, i.e., (Δt).

e_{e0} is the energy in the environment when the closed system is defined at $t = 0$, (i.e., t_0).

33

The change in the environmental energy during the interval from t_0 to t can be expressed as;

$$\Delta e_e = \int_0^t [\dot{e}_w(\tau) - \dot{e}_a(\tau)] \, d\tau \qquad (3.19)$$

Substituting equation 3.19 into equation 3.18 obtains,

$$e_e = e_{e0} + \int_0^t [\dot{e}_w(\tau) - \dot{e}_a(\tau)] \, d\tau \qquad (3.20)$$

The energy in the substance can be expressed in a similar form to that of the environmental energy and is given by;

$$e_s = e_{s0} + \int_0^t [\dot{e}_a(\tau) - \dot{e}_w(\tau)] \, d\tau \qquad (3.21)$$

Where, e_{s0} is the energy in the substance when the closed system is defined at $t=0$.

Equations 3.20 and 3.21 allow the determination of changes in the energies of the substance and the environment as a function of time, that is, the dynamic energy exchange between the substance and its environment.

Substances tend to be in equilibrium with the environment when considered on a reasonable long period of time. For example, a mature substance will have approximately a constant energy content over relatively long periods of time. For equilibrium conditions, the amount of energy accepted by, and the amount of energy released by a substance are equal, and the energy of the substance is not changing. However, a substance can experience changes in its energy, for example, during periods of growth in living substances and during periods when the accepted or released energy changes due to environmental factors, the energy of the substance will change, i.e., Δe_s will not be zero.

The energy released by a substance is not directly related to accepted energy; the relationship between these energies being related through the energy of the substance. For example,

34

the metabolic rate of an animal is essentially the same whether food energy is being accepted by the animal or stored energy in the animal is being used for the metabolic process. The general functions of the substance-environment energy system can be represented by a block diagram as shown in Figure 3-8. The environmental energy is operated on by the energy acceptance process of the substance which results in the substance accepting energy at a rate ($\dot{e}_a$). This accepted energy causes the energy of the substance to increase. The energy release process of the substance operates on the energy of the substance causing this energy to decrease and results in a flow of energy from the substance to the environment.

The substance-environment energy system can be expressed in functional form as shown in Figure 3-9 by using the proper functional form in the block diagram. The energy accepted by a substance is a function of the type, form, and level of the

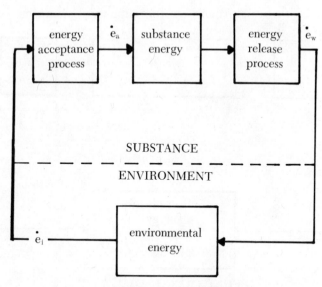

BLOCK DIAGRAM
SUBSTANCE-ENVIRONMENT ENERGY SYSTEM

Figure 3-8

environment energy and of the substance's characteristics, and its energy. Therefore, the energy acceptance process in the block diagram (Figure 3-8) can be expressed in functional notation as f_a (e_s, e_e). As an example of the dependence of the energy acceptance process on environmental energy, a green plant accepts environmental energy in the form of radiant solar energy, carbon dioxide, and water as contrasted with non green plants which accept environmental energy in the form of carbohydrates. As an example of the dependence of the energy acceptance process on the substance's energy form and level, animals have the capability of obtaining energy from only certain types of food due to its particular method of processing these foods.

The process for the release of energy from a substance to the environment is also a function of the energy in the environ-

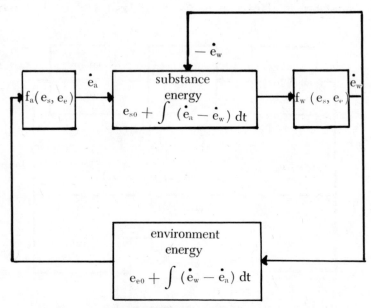

FUNCTIONAL DIAGRAM
SUBSTANCE-ENVIRONMENT ENERGY SYSTEM

Figure 3-9

36

ment, and the energy and characteristics of the substance. The functional relationship for the energy release process can be expressed as f_w (e_s, e_e).

The functional form of the substance's energy and the energy of the environment can be expressed as;

$$e_s = e_{s0} + \int (\dot{e}_a - \dot{e}_w)\, dt$$

and
$$e_e = e_{s0} + \int (\dot{e}_w - \dot{e}_a)\, dt \qquad \text{respectively.}$$

Expressing the block diagram given in Figure 3-8 in functional form obtains the functional diagram in Figure 3-9.

3.5 Directed Energy

The energy in an energy system which is acted upon by a substance is called directed energy. In general, the energy directed by a substance has been changed from one form of energy to another, or has been controlled in some way. Therefore, directed energy can be considered as being regulated, controlled, guided or otherwise processed or changed by a substance.

In Paragraph 3.1, it was shown that the directed energy is a subset of energy in both the substance and the environment. To develop expressions for directed energy which will allow the computation and measurement of directed energy, it is necessary to determine the form of the directed energy in the substance and the environment, and to determine the nature of the energy which flows between the substance and its environment by the direction of the substance. Directed energy expressions are developed below for the directed energy in the substance and in the environment at a given instant of time. By considering the directed energy at a given instant of time and assuming the interface between the substance and the environment to be infinitely thin, the directed energy can be determined by calculating the directed energy in the substance and in the environment. The flow of energy between the substance and the environment can be neglected for an infinitely

37

thin interface and an infinitely short period of time. Expressions are also developed for directed energy in a small interval of time in order to account for the exchange of energy between the substance and the environment.

Substance Internal Directed Energy

It might seem at first thought that all the energy of the substance at a given instant of time has been operated on in some way and hence is directed energy. However, the energy of the substance, as given in equation 3.12, includes energies which are not directed by the substance; for example, the mass energy of the nuclear components which make up the substance is not changed or acted upon by the substance. To illustrate this point, consider the following example. A living substance is composed of many atoms of different matter. During the lifetime of the living substance, the mass energy of the atoms making up the living substance is not changed or altered in any way; i.e., the atomic energy of the substance, as represented by the well known Einstein equation, $E = mc^2$, has not been changed or directed by the substance in any way.

The nature of the directed internal energy of a substance can be seen by considering one of the simplest molecules; i.e., a diatomic molecule. A solution of appropriate equations from the theory of wave mechanics indicate that the total energy of a diatomic molecule consist of three parts: 1) the energy of the original atoms; 2) coulombic energy resulting from the electrostatic attraction between the electrons and the nuclei; 3) exchange energy (References 3.1 and 3.2). The solution gives two expressions for the total energy as a function of separation distance between the two nuclei. One solution represents a stable molecule, the other an unstable molecule. These solutions are shown as curve A and B respectively in Figure 3-10. As the nuclei are brought together as shown by curve A in Figure 3-10, the attraction between the nuclei increase until a point r_0 is reached where the attraction is

38

maximum. A stable normal molecule will have a separation distance of r_0 between the two nuclei, the distance r_0 being different for different diatomic molecules.

The total potential energy E of the molecule (see Figure 3-10) consists of the electronic energy e_{se}, the vibrational energy e_{sv}, the rotational energy e_{sh}, and the energy of thermal motion e_{sT}; i.e.,

$$E = e_{se} + e_{sv} + e_{sh} + e_{sT}. \qquad (3.22)$$

At zero degrees absolute temperature, both e_{sh} and e_{sT} are zero, and e_{sv} reduces to the zero point energy of the molecule, i.e., $E_0 = \frac{1}{2}h\nu_0$. Therefore, at absolute zero the energy is given by

$$[E_{T=0}] = e_{se} + \frac{1}{2}h\nu_0 \qquad (3.23)$$

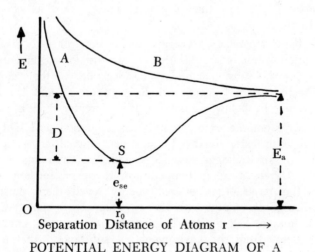

POTENTIAL ENERGY DIAGRAM OF A
DIATOMIC MOLECULE

Figure 3-10

which is shown as point S in Figure 3-10. In equation 3.23, h is Planck's constant and ν_0 is the fundamental vibrational frequency of the molecule.

The energy level E_a in Figure 3-10 is the total energy required to cause the molecule to dissociate into its component atoms. The difference between the lowest energy state e_{se} and the dissociation energy E_a, namely D in Figure 3-10, is the energy range of a stable molecule. That is, the molecule can exist between the energy level e_{se} and E_a. When the energy level E_a is reached, our substance, the diatomic molecule, ceases to exist but the atomic energy remains unchanged.

In our example, e_{se} is the minimum energy of the molecule. When the two atoms of the molecule dissociate, there is less organization and a higher energy level of the two atoms. When electrons are stripped from the atom, there is still less organization but higher internal (potential) energy of the atom. The total energy increases as more elementary particles are brought together to form this higher organized substance; however, the process of organization causes the total energy of the substance to be less than the total energy of the collective individuals.

The basic organization energy in the example is e_{se}; where basic organization energy is defined as the lowest amount of energy for the substance under consideration. In the example, the directed internal energy can lie between e_{se} and E_a. That is, it cannot be below e_{se} nor can it be greater than E_a.

We see from the example and from equation 3.23 that the molecule can exist in the basic organizational state in the absence of an exchange of energy with the environment; i.e., at zero degrees absolute temperature. However, for any state above the basic organizational energy level, there must be an exchange of energy with the environment to maintain the higher internal energy level. In the absence of a continual input energy from the environment, a substance will tend to approach the minimum energy condition.

It is convenient to consider the internal directed energy as permanent, semipermanent, and transient. The permanent directed energy is the basic organizational energy. Indeed, if the energy were to drop below the basic organizational energy, the substance would cease to exist. Therefore, the permanent directed energy will exist as long as the substance exists. The semipermanent directed internal energy is the difference between the basic organizational energy level and the "normal" internal energy level for the normal environment of the substance. This energy can be increased or decreased as a function of changes in the environment. The transient internal energy is the energy which passes through the substance in some reasonable small period of time. The transient energy is required to keep the internal energy at some given operating point. Any substance will release energy in trying to approach its lower energy state, the amount of energy released is a function of the type of substance. Transient energy from the environment is required to replace the energy released to the environment.

The permanent and the semipermanent energy can be considered as internal potential energy of the substance. Both these energies are directed by the substance. The transient energy is also directed by the substance.

The internal energy of polyatomic molecules is much more complicated than for a diatomic molecule. However, the principles of internal energy or directed internal energy apply equally well to diatomic and polyatomic molecules. More complex substances such as aggregates of molecules, living cells, tissue, organs, and organisms, exhibit much more complicated internal energy arrangements. The directed internal energy is discussed in more detail in following chapters which deal with these more complex substances.

A particular energy form, such as mechanical or chemical energy may or may not be present in a given substance. These energies may or may not be directed energies depending again on the type of substance. A more detailed discussion of this type directed energy is considered in later chapters. It should be noted that the internal directed energy considered above is for a particular instant of time.

41

Directed Enviromental Energy

Many substances are capable of directing environmental energy. The directed environmental energy could have any of the forms of environmental energy given Paragraph 3.3. The amount and form of directed environmental energy is determined by the type of substance being considered. Due to the directed energy being so dependent on the type and form of the substance, general directed environmental energy relations applicable to all substances are precluded. Directed environmental energy relationships are considered in more detail in the chapters on types of substances, namely minerals, plants, and animals.

Although general directed environmental energy relations applicable to all substances are not meaningful, it is appropriate to consider certain directed environmental energy relations. It is convenient to consider the directed environmental energy as being either potential or dynamic energy. Potential energy is defined as energy which is stored and having the potential to perform work. Dynamic energy is defined as an energy flow rate.

Some substances are capable of directing potential energy in the environment. This potential energy can be in the form of stored foods, water, oxidizers, heat, mechanical energy, etc. The energy in food, water, and oxidizers is usually utilized by a living substance in the form of chemical energy. Likely forms of directed environmental energy are chemical, heat, and mechanical energies. When a particular substance has been specified, its capability for directing the afore mentioned forms of potential energy can be determined and the directed potential environmental energy obtained by the addition of the directed energy of the various forms.

All substances direct dynamic energy either within itself or within the environment or both between itself and the environment. As this energy is dynamic, it is in the form of an energy flow as a function of time, i.e., an energy flow rate.

Consider the dynamic energy in the environment that is directed by a substance but is not interchanged between the substance and the environment. The most general form of this type environmental energy is that which impinges upon the substance but is rejected by the substance. This rejected energy is directed by the substance as the flow of energy is caused to change direction by the substance. An example of this directed energy is solar radiant energy which is reflected by a substance. The solar energy in the environment impinges upon the substance, through no effort by the substance, but the substance, in general, will have selective absorption and reflection properties at its surface and hence will reflect, i.e., redirect, some of the energy.

The environmental energy which has been rejected by the substance can be in the form of an energy flux which changes with time, such as solar energy at some particular location on earth, that is, a rate of energy flow which changes with time. Let this rejected energy flow be denoted by

$$\dot{e}_r = \frac{de_r}{dt} \quad , \tag{3.24}$$

where $\dot{e}_r$ is a function of time. Then in a small increment of time, dt, the substance rejects; i.e., directs, an amount of environmental energy given by the following equation;

$$de_r = \dot{e}_r dt \quad . \tag{3.25}$$

If the rejected energy is desired over a longer period of time, for instance a diurnal cycle, it can be obtained from the following equation:

$$e_r = \int_{t_1}^{t_2} \dot{e}_r dt \tag{3.26}$$

where, $(t_2 - t_1)$ is the time interval of interest.

The amount of directed environmental energy can be obtained when the substance and the local environment are specified. The reflection properties of the particular substance must be specified and the environmental energy impinging on the substance must be specified or determined as a function of time.

These properties will be treated in more detail in later chapters.

Some substances can direct other forms of dynamic energies such as thermal, wind, etc. These directed energies can be treated in the same manner as the rejected radiant energy with equations of a form similar to 3.25 and 3.26, i.e.,

$$de_{de} = \dot{e}_{de}dt.$$

Directed Substance-Environment Exchange Energy

Expressions for the energy exchange between a substance and its environment were developed in Paragraph 3.4. We wish now to determine the amount of this dynamic energy that is directed by the substance. Some of the energy which flows through the substance is not changed either in the substance or in the environment and hence is not directed energy. Mass energy is an example of energy flow which is not directed by the substance. A careful distinction must be made between the energy in the substance and that in the environment when the energy flow across the interface between the substance and the environment in an interval of time is considered; otherwise the energy flowing across the interface could be counted twice as directed energy. The possible difficulty in counting directed energy more than once can be alleviated by applying elementary set theory. As in equation 3.6, we will assume the directed energy is composed of a part that is contained in the environment and a part that is contained in the substance. In addition, we will define $e_{ds}e_{de}$ as the directed energy that lies in both the substance and the environment. This energy, $e_{ds}e_{de}$, is that which flows from the environment to the substance and from the substance to the environment in the interval of time Δt. Utilizing set theory notation, we obtain the following expression for directed energy in a time interval Δt;

$$e_d = e_{ds} + e_{de} - e_{ds}e_{de} \tag{3.27}$$

If we let e_{dd} be the directed dynamic energy which flows through the substance, then from Figure 3-6 and the equations in Paragraph 3.4, we have that;

$$de_{dd} = de_a + de_w - de_a de_w \qquad (3.28)$$

That is, the directed dynamic energy through the substance is equal to the energy accepted in the time interval Δt plus the substance energy which performs work on the environment in time Δt minus the energy which flows through the interface between the substance and the environment in this time interval.

There may be additional dynamic energies which are internal to a substance such as the potential energy which has been converted to dynamic energy; conversion of fats into heat and mechanical energy is an example of this type dynamic energy. In general, this type energy is directed by the substance. Howewer, a precise determination can only be made on a case by case basis.

Total Directed Energy

The total directed energy is the sum of the individual potential and dynamic energies in the substance and in the environment and is given symbolically by equation 3.9. A detailed development of the directed energy of a substance must wait until the various kinds of substances are considered. So far we have considered some general forms of the types of energies. These forms are expanded and detailed more specifically in later chapters.

3.6 *General Characteristics of Substances*

In the preceding material, a substance has been defined and some of the equations relating to its energy discussed; however, the characteristics of substances as they relate to knowledge were not addressed. Some general characteristics of substances, as they relate to knowledge, is the topic of this paragraph.

A basic postulate relating to a substance and knowledge is:

45

When energy takes form, it acquires the attribute of knowledge.

A substance's knowledge is a function of its basic characteristics. These basic characteristics are considered below, proceeding from simple to more sophisticated characteristics and substances.

The most basic characteristics of any substance are the minimum energy and knowledge required for the substance to maintain its identity. That is, the minimum energy and knowledge required for the substance to survive. The knowledge and energy required for survival varies from substance to substance. The minimum knowledge and energy required for a substance to survive is, in general, a well defined point and is a characteristic of the substance. Substances can be considered by their gross organizational structures and the energy required for survival.

The basic substances of the universe, such as the physical elements, can survive in the absence of energy from the environment. The directed energy required for the survival of these elements is the energy associated with the minimum electronic energy of the substance. This ground state energy is given by equation 3.23 and is the lowest energy level at which any substance can survive (exist). It is of interest to note that this survival energy level does not change with time, i.e., it is a steady state condition.

The more sophisticated substances such as plants and animals require rather elaborate energy systems and methods of exchanging energy with the environment. These substances must have not only ground state potential energy and have a thermal energy exchange with the environment, but must have a mass exchange with the environment in order to survive. These sophisticated processes for controlling energy allow these subtances to obtain sufficient energy for survival, however after a period of time the substance, i.e., plants and animals, die from "natural causes". The minimum energy required for these substances to survive is rather well defined.

To survive, substances must have sufficient knowledge to reject energies which exceed values that would cause the substance to change state, i.e., to expire. The energy level which causes a substance to expire is a basic characteristic of the particular substance. Energy in different forms will have different effects on a substance depending on such basic properties of the substance as selective rejection of energies at the surface, selective transmission of energies through the substance and selective absorption of energies by the substance. The maximum levels of the various types of energy, i.e., radiant, mechanical, electrical, chemical, etc., which cause a substance to expire can be determined. If a substance is to survive in a given environment, it must be capable of rejecting all energy above the maximum tolerable level.

Let $\dot{\alpha}$ be the total environmental energy flow rate that is directed toward, impinges upon, or interfaces with the sub-

stance, and let $\dot{e}_s]_{max}$ be the maximum energy flow rate that can be tolerated by the substance. The energy flow which must be rejected $(\dot{e}_r)_s$ by the substance if it is to survive is given by:

$$(\dot{e}_r)_s = \dot{\alpha} - \dot{e}_s]_{max} .$$

The energy which must be directed is;

$$d(e_r)_s = d\alpha - de_s]_{max} \tag{3.29}$$

The knowledge required for a substance to survive can be determined based on the survival characteristics of the substance.

The basic substances (elements) must have sufficient knowledge to direct internal energy of magnitude given by equation 3.23 and must have sufficient knowledge to reject an amount of energy given by equation 3.29.

To survive, all substances must possess sufficient knowledge to (1) direct the minimum internal energy characteristic of the particular substance, (2) direct energy exchange at the interface (dynamic energy) to maintain the substance's internal energy, and (3) reject energy at the interface that will exceed the maximum energy capability of the substance.

The conditions on the energy exchange at the interface are such that, in general, there must be an energy balance.

Otherwise, minimum energy conditions are not maintained. The survival knowledge of a substance is determined by obtaining all the directed energy required for the substance to survive and then applying the basic knowledge equation; $k = Se_d$.

The basic knowledge equation, as given in equation 3.3, is valid for a range of knowledge from 0 to e_t. The range of energy levels over which equation 3.3 is valid for a particular substance can now be stated based on the substance's survival knowledge. Equation 3.3 and its range is as follows for a particular substance;

$$k = Se_d , \quad \text{for} \quad k_s \leqq k \leqq Se_t \quad (3.30)$$

where k_s is the survival knowledge and is related to the directed survival energy of the substances. The directed energy required for the survival of a particular substance depends on the characteristics of that particular substance. The curve shown in Figure 3-3 is modified as shown in Figure 3-11 when the survival knowledge of a substance is considered.

Figure 3-11 is a plot of equation 3.30.

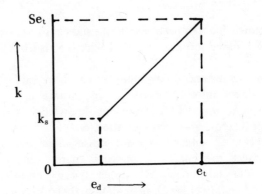

KNOWLEDGE vs DIRECTED ENERGY:
SURVIVAL LIMITED

Figure 3-11

*3.7 Information

A discussion of knowledge theory would not be complete without a consideration of information. Although I have changed the concept of knowledge, there is no need to change the concept of information as the standard definition, namely the communication of knowledge, is completly satisfactory. However, the interpretation of information may change slightly. A few examples are given below to illustrate the usage of information in connection with the theory of knowledge presented herein.

Example # 1, Substance to offspring: Living organisms pass information to their offsprings which provide the offpring with sufficient knowledge to form energy in such a way that it has the same basic characteristics as the parents. The offspring has been given sufficient information so that it can direct approximately the same amount of both substance and environmental energy as the parent. The methods of transferring this information is a study discipline in itself, i.e., genetics.

Example # 2, Environment to substance: Changes in the environment of a substance may cause a substance to acquire additional knowledge. In this case, the substance obtained information about the environment which caused the substance to assimilate this information and hence possess additional knowledge.

Example # 3, Substance to substance: Some living organisms have the capability of communicating knowledge from one individual to another. That is, one substance can, by the transmittal of information, cause another substance to direct more energy and hence have increased knowledge. This particular example is more nearly akin to the normal concept of information.

*3.7.1 Information Theory and Knowledge

Information theory is related to the process of communication. The theory treats the maximum speed and accuracy of communication that can be achieved with a given communication transmission facility. The measure of information in information theory is not concerned with the meaning or purpose of communication. Information in this sense is concerned with a set of possible answers. When some information is gained, the number of possible answers is reduced. Complete information, as it pertains to communication systems, is a function of the ratio of possible answers before and after information is available.

Information theory, based on the classical investigations of C. E. Shannon, is concerned with the transmission of symbols (see, for instance, *Information Theory* by S. Goldman; Reference 3.3). The average amount of information per symbol, as obtained from information theory, can be expressed as:

$$H(x) = - \sum_{i}^{n} p_i \text{Log } p_i$$

where p_i is the probability of occurrence of the ith symbol. This equation for the amount of information contained in a specific arrangement of symbols has the same form as the statistical mechanics equation used by Boltzmann and Gibbs to describe entropy. In statistical mechanics, entropy provides a measure of disorder, maximum entropy corresponding to complete disorder. Based on the work of Shannon, it has been demonstrated that information corresponds to negative entropy.

The definition of entropy was first developed in connection with the amount of work that can be obtained from a closed thermodynamic system. In this context, entropy is defined in relationship to the energy in the system which is not available to perform work. The concept of entropy in the thermodynamic sense is explained in nontechnical terms by Erwin Schrödinger in his book WHAT IS LIFE? (Reference 3.4). I quote "at the absolute zero point of temperature (roughly $-273°C.$) the entropy of any substance is zero. When you bring the substance into any other state by slow, reversible little steps (even if thereby the substance changes its physical or chemical nature) the entropy increases by an amount which is computed by dividing every little portion of heat you had to supply in that proceduce by the absolute temperature at which it was supplied and by summing up all these small contributions. To give an example, when you melt a solid, its entropy increases by the amount of the heat of fusion divided by the temperature at the melting-point. You see from this, that the unit in which entropy is measured is Cal./°C."

In the statistical sense, entropy can be expressed as:

$$\text{entropy} = k \text{ Log } D,$$

where k is Boltzmann's constant (3.2983×10^{-24} cal. per degree centegrade) and D is a measure of the atomic disorder of the substance under investigation.

As information theory deals with the ordering and transmission of symbols, it is not related to the measure of knowledge as presented in this book. That is, information theory does not allow a determination of directed energy. Indeed, the amount of information determined from information theory is the same for a theorem by Einstein or a random assemblage of letters provided the number of letters is the same.

*3.7.2 Entropy, Order, and Knowledge

The concept of information and order has been considered by various authors in areas other than communication systems. Two notable areas are the information of a particular machine organization and the information of biological organizations. The basic concept of information, i.e., negentropy, as applied to machines and biological organisms is that they consist of a number of elements and that their negentropy (information) is a measure of the probability that their elements are in a specific order or arrangement, given that all the other possible arrangements of these elements are equally probable.

Information related to order can be expressed as;

$$I = k \text{ ln } P_0$$

where k is Beltzmann's constant with a value of 1.38×10^{-16} in ergs per degree centigrade, and P_0 is the possible number of outcomes of all arrangements of elements. Information obtained by this equation is in entropy units. Therefore, the information of any specific organization can be expressed in entropy units. For example, the information of a telephone network with 10^8 subscribers can be calculated to be 4×10^{-7}.

As information, i.e., negentropy, is related to entropy which in turn is a quality or grade of energy, one might suspect that negentropy could represent directed energy. However, it is not clear to me that a relationship exists between entropy and directed energy or knowledge.

Erwin Schrödinger in his book WHAT IS LIFE? applied the concept of negentropy to living things. The major conclusions reached by Schrödinger is that order is based on order in living substances and that organization is maintained in living substances by sucking order from the environment. That is, living substances feed from negentropy. André Lwoff in his book BIOLOGICAL ORDER (Reference 3.5) takes issue with the negentropy concept as presented by Schrödinger and as extended by Brillouin (Rerefence 3.6). The major argument presented by Lwoff is that functional order is essential to living systems but that this funcional order cannot be measured in terms of entropy units. One argument presented by Lwoff against the negentropy approach of Schrödinger and Brillouin is that a lethal mutation in a living system does not change the negentropy of the system even though the system will die and therefore its information destroyed.

Lwoff presents the argument that unless work is produced, it is meaningless to speak of free energy and its entropic component. In addition, he states that energy of high grade, "such as the energy of light or of a chemical bond, cannot be subdivided into positive and negative entropy". Lwoff concludes his argument by stating that "Negentropy is a grade of energy. Orderliness is a probability. The organism does not handle concepts of grade or logarithms of probabilities. The organism handles atoms or molecules and the energy of light or of chemical bonds."

The negentropy and order approach to biological order

present unsurmountable problems for the biologist. I feel that the concept of knowledge presented in this book can overcome the difficulties encountered by the biologist in the areas of biological order, knowledge, and information.

Chapter IV

MEASUREMENT OF KNOWLEDGE

4.0 *Introduction*

To measure knowledge, it is necessary to establish units of measure and to establish values for the parameters in the fundamental equation of knowledge. A value for the total energy in a standard reference energy system is developed and a system of units is presented in this chapter. The merits of absolute and relative limits of knowledge are discussed and the preferable method selected. A standard for the environmental energy is selected and the value of energy for this standard is computed. Methods of measuring the energies and knowledge of substances are presented.

4.1 *Knowledge Units*

A measure of knowledge, as with other basic systems of measure, require a unit of measure. Any unit of measure should fulfill a utility criterion, i.e., it must be useful for the things to be measured. A unit of knowledge related to the total energy in a system could be selected by choosing a value of S which would make k equal to one in the basic knowledge equation (3.3) when the directed energy is equal to the total energy in the system (e_t). However such a system of units will cause any value of knowledge for the usual substances of interest to us to have extremely small values and would cause the unit to depend on the total energy of some arbitrarily defined energy system. It will be more convenient to select another unit for knowledge. As knowledge is related to directed energy, it is desirable to have a basic unit of knowledge tied to a fundamental unit of energy. A unit of knowledge which is directly related to a fundamental unit of energy is a natural unit in the sense that additional definitions and constraints are not required. For these reasons, the basic unit of knowledge will be defined in terms of the basic energy unit. Either the metric, i.e., centimeter-gram-second, or the English, i.e., foot-pound-second system, could be used. The metric system will be used as it is the most universally accepted.

The unit of knowledge is defined as; *one unit of knowledge is required for a substance to direct one Joule of energy.* Therefore, when k is one knowledge unit and the directed energy e_d is one Joule, the constant S is equal to one. The units of S are;

$$S = \frac{1 \text{ knowledge unit}}{1 \text{ Joule}} = \text{Joule}^{-1}.$$

This unit of knowledge measure is independent of the energy system. The unit is equally valid in a small local energy system and a large energy system.

When knowledge is expressed in knowledge units, the equation for knowledge becomes;

$$k = e_d \quad \text{knowledge units} \tag{4.1}$$

where directed energy, e_d, is in Joules and it is understood that the directed energy cannot exceed the total energy in the energy system and that the total energy is effectively constant.

As the directed energy of some substances of interest will be very large, it will probably be desirable to utilize another unit which represents a larger amount of directed energy, e.g.. a kilo Joule. The desirability of such a unit is based on ease of usage and should await the development of directed energy values which will be most useful for a given area of investigation.

4.2 *Absolute vs Relative Limits of Knowledge*

The most desirable upper limit of knowledge would be one suitable for all substances of the universe. The total energy for this absolute knowledge-energy system would contain all the energy in the universe and would give an absolute upper limit of knowledge. Unfortunately, the total energy in the universe is not presently known and may possibly never be known. Therefore an absolute upper limit of knowledge cannot be measured and it may never be possible to measure this knowledge. In the absence of an absolute measure of the total energy in the universe, it is desirable to select a closed energy system such that the environmental energy is sufficiently large to provide an upper limit of knowledge for all substances of interest.

The energy in the solar planetary system could be used as a standard for environmental energy. However, I feel that a closed energy system embodying the entire solar system would contain more energy and result in larger numbers than necessary for our purposes.

An energy system which includes the earth, the moon, and the energy flowing into and out of a space volume which includes the earth and the moon should provide an energy system that can be used as a standard for all substances of interest. Man may be an exception if he expands his environment to include energies from some of the other planets of the solar system. We shall use the energy of the earth, moon and the energy flow into and out of a space volume enclosing the earth and moon as the standard closed energy system which will be used as an upper limit when comparing the knowledge of various substances. This closed energy system is arbitrary, but it does provide a reasonable upper limit for the total energy which can be influenced by known substances.

4.3 *The Standard Closed Energy System*

The standard closed energy system selected above, i.e., the earth, the moon, and the energy flow into and out of a space volume enclosing the earth and the moon, contains such a large amount of energy compared to any given substance that the substance energy can be neglected in the determination of the total energy the energy system. Symbolically, this statement is given as;

$$e_t = e_e = 1/C \quad , \quad \text{where} \quad e_e >> e_s \ .$$

The value of the energy in the standard environment and hence the total energy in the standard energy system can be obtained by using equation 3.12 and 3.14. We have defined the standard energy system to be all the energy in a space volume that includes the earth and the moon. We will further define the space volume to be a cube which is 4.78×10^5 miles on a side with the earth located at the center of the cube. The size of the cube was selected so that the moon would be included in the volume irrespective of its location in its orbit around the earth. The substances to be used in equation 3.14 to determine the energy of the standard energy system are the moon, the earth and all the substances on or in the earth and moon. The radiant energy to be used in equation 3.14 is all the radiant energy in the standard space volume. The majority of the radiant energy is in the form of solar energy.

The energy of the substances in our standard space volume can be determined from equation 3.12. The major energy contributions of the environmental substances to the standard energy are due to the mass, thermal, radiant, and mechanical energies. The value of e_e for the standard environment is readily obtained as we know the mass, temperature, and mechanical energy of the earth and moon, and we know the energy flux through a space volume enclosing the earth and the moon, and the relative velocity of the system. The value of e_e is calculated as follows:

Mass energy: The mass energy of the earth is obtained from the Einstein equation $E = mc^2$. The mass of the earth is given in Reference 4.1 as 5.983×10^{24} kilograms and the velocity of light is 3×10^{10} centimeters per second. The mass energy of the earth is then computed as follows;

$$e_m = (5.98 \times 10^{27} g) \ (3 \times 10^{10} \ cm/sec)^2 \ (10^{-7} \ Joules/erg)$$
$$= 54 \times 10^{40} \ Joules$$

The mass energy of the moon is calculated in the same way as the mass energy of the earth. The mass of the moon (Refer-

58

ence 4.1) is 7.3474×10^{22} kilograms. The mass energy of the moon is;

$$e_m = (7.3474 \times 10^{25}g)\ (3 \times 10^{10}cm/sec)^2\ (10^{-7}\ Joules/erg)$$
$$= 6.61 \times 10^{39}\ Joules.$$

Thermal energy: A substance's thermal energy is a function of its mass (m), specific heat (C), temperature (T), and the amount of heat absorbed during a change of state, i.e., latent heat (L). The thermal energy of a substance is given by the equation;

$$e_{sT} = mCT + \sum_{i=0}^{n} L_i \qquad (4.2)$$

The development of the thermal energy equation is given in almost any standard physics text such as Reference 4.2.

To determine the thermal energy of the earth and the moon, it is necessary to know specific heat and the temperature of the materials that make up the earth and the moon. In addition, it is necessary to know the latent heats of these substances. As none of these characteristics are known with a high degree of certainty, the thermal energy of the earth and the moon cannot be determined precisely. The earth is generally considered to have a spherical iron core with a 3,500 kilometer radius; this core being covered by a dunite shell which is 2,900 kilometers thick; the dunite shell is covered with a 15 kilometer layer of tachylyte or diorite which in turn is covered with an 18 kilometer layer of granite (Reference 4.3). The core of the earth is thought to be in a liquid state with a density of from 9.9 to 12. The mean density of the earth is about 5.5. The core of the earth is considered to have a temperature of approximately 1500 degrees Centigrade, i.e., approximately the temperature of liquid iron.

Let us assume that the specific heat of the earth is the same as iron, namely 0.2 calories/degree, that the temperature is 1500 degrees Centigrade, that the latent heat of fusion, L, is about that of iron, i.e., 5.5 calories per gram, and the mass of the earth is 5.983×10^{27} grams. Then the thermal energy of the earth is given as;

$$e_{eT} = (5.983 \times 10^{27} \text{ gr}) \; [(0.2 \text{ cal/deg}) \; (1773^\circ \text{K}) + 5.5]$$
$$= 2.15 \times 10^{30} \text{ calories, or } 8.99 \times 10^{30} \text{ Joules.}$$

A comparison of the thermal energy of the earth with the mass energy calculated previously shows that the mass energy of the earth is approximately eleven orders of magnitude greater than the thermal energy and therefore the thermal energy can be neglected.

The thermal energy of the moon is also very small in comparison to the mass energy of the moon and therefore can be neglected.

It is concluded that the thermal energy of the earth and the moon do not contribute significantly to the standard environmental energy.

Radiant energy: The radiant energy in the reference space volume at some time t may be due to solar energy, cosmic energy, galactic radiant energy, etc. This radiant energy is actually flowing through the reference space volume; however, for our purpose, it can be assumed that this radiant energy has a constant value and that solar radiation is the major portion of the radiant energy. It is further assumed, for ease of calculation, that the radiant energy from the sun enters one face of the cube, that is, this face is perpendicular to the direction of the radiant energy flux.

We can calculate the radiant energy in the reference volume by finding the area of one face, knowing the time for a wave of energy to completly traverse the volume, and the energy flux in the reference space. The area of one face of the reference space is;

$$A = (7.65 \times 10^{10})^2 = 58.5 \times 10^{20} \text{ cm}^2.$$

The energy entering one face will pass through the reference space in time

$$t = \left[\frac{D}{c} \right] = \left[\frac{4.78 \times 10^5 \text{ miles}}{1.86 \times 10^5 \text{ miles/sec}} \right] = 2.57 \text{ sec.}$$

60

Where D is the length of one side the cube. The energy flux from the sun as measured in the vicinity of the earth is 2 calories/cm²/min or 0.033 calories/cm²/sec. (Reference 4.1). The radiant energy in the reference space environment is;

$$e_{ez} = (0.033 \text{ cal/cm}^2\text{/sec}) \ (58.5 \times 10^{20} \text{ cm}^2) \ (2.57 \text{ sec})$$
$$= 5 \times 10^{20} \text{ calories, or } 20.9 \times 10^{20} \text{ Joules.}$$

This radiant energy is very small as compared to the thermal energy and to the mass energy, hence it can be neglected.

Mechanical energy: The significant mechanical energy in the reference space environment is due to the rotation of the moon about the earth. The rotation of the earth about the sun and the motion of the galactic system are excluded from the reference system by the way we defined the reference space environment.

The approximate mechanical energy in the reference environment due to the earth rotation can be obtained by making a few simplifying assumptions. It will be assumed that the earth is a homogeneous sphere with uniformly distributed mass of 5.983×10^{27} grams and radius (r) of 6.37×10^8 cms (Reference 4.1). The mechanical energy due to the earth's rotation is;

$$e_{ek} = \tfrac{1}{2} I \omega^2$$

where $I = (2/5) m \, r^2$, i.e., the moment of inertia, and ω is the angular velocity of the earth. Under these assumptions, the energy due to the earth's rotation is;

$$e_{ek} = (1/5) \ (5.983 \times 10^{27} \text{ gr}) \ (6.37 \times 10^8 \text{ cm})^2 \times$$

$$\left[\frac{2 \pi}{24 \text{ hr. } (3600 \text{ sec/hr})} \right]^2$$

$$= 25.6 \times 10^{35} \text{ ergs or } 25.7 \times 10^{28} \text{ Joules.}$$

The mechanical energy due to rotation of the earth is small compared to the mass energy of the earth and can be neglected. The approximate mechanical energy in our reference environment due to the rotation of the moon about the earth can be obtained by making a few simplifying assumptions. It is assumed that the moon is a point mass of 7.35×10^{25} grams at a distance (r) of 3.8×10^{10} cms (Reference 4.1) and an angular velocity (ω) of 2π radians per 28 days. The energy due to the moon rotating about the earth is given by;

$$e_{ek} = \tfrac{1}{2} I \, \omega^2$$

where; $I = mr^2$. The rotational energy is computed to be;

$$e_{ek} = \tfrac{1}{2} (1.06 \times 10^{47}) \left[\frac{2\pi}{28 \times 24 \times 3600} \right]^2 = 3.58 \times 10^{35} \text{ ergs}$$

$$= 3.58 \times 10^{28} \text{ Joules}$$

This energy is seen to be small compared to the mass energy of the earth.

Reference environmental energy value: The total energy in the reference environment is the sum of the energies calculated in the foregoing paragraphs. We have for the reference environment;

$$e_e = [54 \times 10^{40}] + [0.66 \times 10^{40}] + [8.99 \times 10^{30}] + [21 \times 10^{20}]$$
$$+ [2.5 \times 10^{29}] + [3.6 \times 10^{28}] \text{ Joules.}$$

$$e_e = 54.66 \times 10^{40} \text{ Joules.}$$

The uncertainty in the determination of e_e for the reference environment and the purpose of the reference environment makes it undesirable to carry the value of e_e to more than two significant figures. Therefore we will select a value of e_e and hence e_t to be 5.4×10^{41} Joules.

The fundamental equation of knowledge for the standard total energy system becomes;

$$k = e_d \,, \qquad 0 \leqq e_d \leqq 5.4 \times 10^{41} \text{ Joules} \qquad (4.3)$$

where e_d is expressed in Joules and k is in knowledge units.

*4.4 *Methods of Measurement*

We now have an equation which relates knowledge to directed

energy and a system of units for energy and knowledge. Therefore, we are in a position to determine the amount of energy directed by a substance and hence its knowledge through the use of energy measurement techniques. The directed energy of interest to us can be in the form of physical, chemical, and biological energy. The directed energy of a substance has all the attributes of the energies normally encountered in the physical, chemical, and biological sciences and hence can be measured by the techniques of these sciences. Therefore we can conclude that the measurement of directed energies and the calculation of knowledge from these measurements presents no particular problem.

CHAPTER V

MINERAL KNOWLEDGE

5.0 *Introduction*

A review of the important characteristics of minerals is given herein to provide background for the application of the principles of knowledge to minerals. The review is limited to those characteristics which assist in the identification of a particular mineral species, i.e. substance, and those characteristics which allow the determination of directed energy and knowledge for a mineral. The standard classifications and characteristics of mineralogy, chemistry, and physics will be used to the extent possible.

The word mineral is used herein to identify one of the three major divisions of the universe. That is, the mineral kingdom as opposed to the plant and the animal kingdoms.

The basic principles of knowledge developed in the preceding chapters are applied to minerals in this chapter. The equations developed in the preceding chapters are used in conjunction with the basic characteristics of minerals to develop directed energy and knowledge relations for minerals. An example is given, using hydrogen as the mineral substance, which demonstrates the application of the equations to minerals.

5.1 *Characteristics of Minerals*

In Paragraph 2.0 a substance is defined as anything that has fundamental or characteristic physical and/or chemical properties. It was also stated in Paragraph 2.0 that the substance will continue to exist, i.e., survive, so long as the fundamental properties remain essentially the same. To determine the knowledge of a mineral, we must know some of its fundamental characteristics. Essential mineral characteristics are those relating to chemical composition, crystalline form, crystallo-physical properties and specific gravity; these are identical, or vary only within certain defined limits, in all specimens of the same mineral-species. Nonessential characters, e.g. color, luster, hardness, form and structure of aggregates, depend largely on the presence of impurities, or on the state of aggregation of imperfectly formed crystalline individuals.

In the following discussion of the important characters of minerals, many of the terms used for nonessential characters are purely descriptive and have no exact definition; however the essential characters can be expressed numerically and are therefore perfectly defined.

5.1.1 *Morphological Characters*

Crystalline form: This important character of minerals can be determined only when the substance is in the form of crystals (i.e., crystallized), which is not always the case. Massive aggregates of crystalline substance occur more frequently in nature than pure crystals.

Crystals of the same mineral-species may differ greatly in general form or habit.; e.g., crystals of calcite may be rhombohedral, prismatic, scalenohedral or tabalar in habit. In addition, the faces of natural crystals may be smooth, rough, striated, curved or drusy, i.e., studded with small crystal faces and angles.

State of Aggregation: Aggregation of a number of imperfectly developed crystals, which have grown together, may present various kinds of structure even in the same mineral species. The descriptive terms applied to these structures are generally self explanatory; thus, the structure may be granular (e.g. marble), fibrous (asbestos), radio-fibrous or stellated (wave-like), columnar (beryl), laminar or lamellar (talc), bladed (kyanite), etc., according to the relative shape and sizes of the individual crystals composing the aggregate. Some minerals are amorphous, i.e., without any crystalline structure, however they are comparatively few in number (e.g. opal). Many which are apparently amorphous are really micro crystalline (e.g. turquoise).

5.1.2 *Physical Characters*

Optical characters: The action of crystallized matter on trans-mitted light is a very important characteristic in mineralogy. Even when the substance is opaque in large masses, it may be sufficiently transparent when in thin sections for the deter-mination of the optical characters. The refractive indices, optic axial angle, strength of the double refraction, extinction angles on certain faces, are constant for each mineral species.

The degree of transparency differs widely even in the same mineral species. Some, such as metals and most metallic sulphides are always opaque; while others may vary in different specimens from perfect transparency to perfect opacity (in the latter case, however, minute sections will, as a rule, still be transparent). A good example of this is afforded by the varieties of quartz; rock crystal being water-clear, while chalcedony is translucent and jasper opaque.

The color of minerals is a character which may vary almost indefinitely in one and the same kind of mineral; it affords a typical example of a nonessential character.

An important characteristic of transparent crystals is that of unequal absorption in different directions; so that light will, in general, have a different color depending on the direction in which it has traveled through the crystal; this phenomenon is known as dichronism or pleochroism. Certain minerals (e.g. Zircon and those containing cerium) when examined with a spectroscope show characteristic absorption spectra.

Thermal characters: The specific heat and melting point of minerals are essential characters capable of exact measurement and numerical expression and, therefore, are of primary impor-tance in the determination of knowledge.

Characters depending on cohesion: In many cases when a crystallized mineral is broken it separates in certain definite directions along plane surfaces. This property of "cleavage"

67

is an important essential character of minerals, and one which is often used to assist in their recognition.

"Hardness", or the resistance which a substance offers to being scratched by a harder body, is an important character of minerals, and is frequently used to assist in their identification. In addition, parting planes, etching figures, pressure and percussion figures are sometimes important in describing and distinguishing minerals.

Specific gravity: The density, or specific gravity, of minerals is an essential character of considerable deterministic value. In minerals of constant composition it has a difinite value, but in isomorphous groups it varies with the composition; it also varies with the purity of the material. It is a character which can be expressed numerically.

Radioactivity: Strong radioactivity of certain minerals provides a ready means of recognition for these ores.

5.1.3 Chemical Characters

Chemical composition is the most important character of minerals and is the basis of all modern systems of classification. However, a mineral species cannot be defined by chemical composition alone, since many instances are known in which the same chemical element or compound is dimorphous or polymorphous. In such cases, a knowledge of some other essential character, preferable the crystalline form, is required before the mineral can be determined.

The principle of isomorphism is of the highest importance in mineralogy for the classification of minerals. In some minerals (e.g. quartz) isomorphous or vicarious replacement is not known to occur; however, in the majority of minerals one or the other of the predominating elements may be isomorphously replaced by equivalent amounts of the chemically related elements.

5.1.4 *Alteration of Minerals: Pseudomorphs*

Crystals which have formed under one set of temperature and pressure conditions and in the presence of certain solutions, will in many cases be unstable under another set of conditions. The crystals may then be corroded or even completely redissolved or the substance may undergo a chemical or physical change resulting in the formation of minerals stable under the new conditions.

Pseudomorphs are frequently found in nature and they are of considerable importance in studying the changes which minerals undergo. There are several kinds of pseudomorphs. If the alteration has not involved a change in chemical composition of the material, but only in the internal crystalline structure and physical properties, the altered crystal is called a "paramorph". For example, aragonite crystals are often altered to a confused granular aggregate of crystalline calcity individuals, the change being accompanied by a decrease in specific gravity but without change in external form. An "epimorph" results from the encrustation of one mineral by another; the first may be partly or wholly dissolved out, leaving the second as a hollow shell (e.g. chalybite after fluor-spar).

5.2 *Nomenclature and Classification of Minerals*

A mineral species, or simple mineral, is completely defined by the specification of its chemical composition and crystalline form. When dealing with a definite chemical compound, the limitation of species is relatively easy; thus, carundum, cassiterite, galena, blend, etc., are well defined mineral species. However, with isomorphous mixtures the division into species, or into sub-species and varieties, must be to a certain extent arbitrary, as there are no sharp lines of demarcation in many isomorphous groups of minerals.

Minerals may be classified in various ways to suit different purposes, e.g., according to their uses, modes of occurrence, system of crystallization, etc. The earlier systematic classifications were based solely on external characters, i.e., on natural history principles and hence are too artificial to be of any value in either classification or in the determination of knowledge. The systematic classifications presently in use are modification in detail of the crystallo-chemical system of G. Rose (1852). This system has four main divisions: elements; sulphides, arsenides, etc.; halogen compounds; and oxygen compounds. The last, and largest, division is subdivided into oxides. The classifications adopted by different authors vary greatly in detail, especially in the large section of the silicates.

We are interested in two major methods of classifying minerals (1) by the essential characters of a substance which identify it as being different from other substances and those characters which allow us to identify major changes in state, and (2) by the energy of the substance and the characters which determine the energy of the substance and the energy interface with the environment.

To identify one mineral species substance from another, we will use the essential characters discussed in Paragraph 5.1. In addition, we are interested in those characters which allow us to determine that a substance has changed state. In our terminology, a change in state is equivalent to the demise of the substance and therefore is a very important character in the theory of knowledge.

The most important essential characters are (1) mass (in terms of some standard, e.g. specific gravity or density), (2) thermal capacity, (3) dissociation energy level, (4) sublimation point, (5) structural organization (i.e., the atomic, molecular, crystalline and aggregate organization of the substance), and (6) the surface absorption and reflection characteristics, i.e., the capability of exchanging energy with the environment. The structural organization characteristic is a combination of the crystallo-physical and chemical classifications as discussed in Pharagraph 5.1.

5.3 Knowledge of Mineral Substances

As this book treats the knowledge of individuals, a mineral individual must be defined. To be consistent with a definition of individuals in the plant and animal kingdoms, the mineral individual must be the smallest recognizable unit of a particular species which retains the essential characteristics of the species, A molecule is defined as the smallest unit quantity of matter which can exist by itself and retain all the properties of the original substance. Therefore, we will define a mineral individual as a molecule of the particular mineral species under consideration.

Many of the minerals encountered in nature are not individuals but are groups of individuals. The mineral aggregates are a good example of mineral groups composed of individuals from different species. Other minerals are often found in nature as groups of identical individuals. It is the knowledge of the individuals in these groups and the individuals which are found free in nature that are treated herein.

5.3.1 *Substance Energy*

The knowledge of an individual mineral substance is related to the directed energy of the substance which in turn is related to the total energy of the substance. Therefore, it is necessary to develop equations for the total energy of a mineral substance and for the portion of this energy which is directed by the substance.

The energy of any substance was derived in Chapter III and expressed by equation 3.12 as;

$$e_s = e_{sm} + e_{sT} + e_{sc} + e_{sk} + \cdots = \sum_j e_{sj}$$

To apply this equation to minerals, it is necessary to relate the energy characteristics of minerals to the terms of this equation. The forms of energy for minerals are well known and are described in most elementary physics books. More detailed treatments of a mineral's energy are given by quantum mechanics theory. From the quantum mechanics theory (Reference 3.1), it is known that the energy of a mineral molecule is due to: (1) the mass of the molecule, (2) the electronic energy, (3) the translational energy of the molecule, (4) molecular vibration, and (5) rotation of the molecule. The equation for the energy of a mineral substance becomes;

$$e_s = e_{sm} + e_{se} + e_{st} + e_{sv} + e_{sh} \qquad (5.1)$$

where; e_{sm} is the mass energy of the molecule
            e_{se} is the electronic energy of the molecule
            e_{st} is the translational energy of the molecule
            e_{sv} is the molecular vibrational energy
            e_{sh} is the molecular rotational energy.

It is beyond the scope of this book to treat the quantum theory of molecular structure and the partition of energy in a molecule. However, a few words are necessary to obtain a qualitative view of a molecule's energy. The energy due to the mass of the molecule is determined by the familiar $E = mc^2$ formula where m is now the mass of the molecule. The electronic energy is due to the location and motion of the electrons about the nuclei of the atoms which constitute the molecule. The translational energy is due to the kinetic energy of the molecule with respect to some reference system. The vibrational energy is due to the vibration of the atoms of a molecule with respect to one another. The rotational energy is due to the rotation of the atoms of the molecule about the rotational axis of the molecule.

The energy of a mineral substance, as given in equation 5.1, can be considered to be composed of three parts; namely, mass energy, translational energy, and internal thermal energy. The internal thermal energy is made up of the electronic, vibrational, and rotational energy of the molecule. The mass energy of the molecule is constant for any mineral species, except for the radioactive minerals, and constitutes a predominant portion of the molecule's energy. The remaining energy of the substance can be related to heat capacity, thermal energy, and zero state electronic energy.

The mass energy of the molecule can be determined by knowing the mass of the particular molecule under consideration. As the mass of a molecule is an essential characteristic with a particular value for a given mineral species, the mass energy can be determined. The zero state electronic energy of a mineral substance is also an essential characteristic of a particular mineral species and can be defined. The heat capacity of a mineral species is an essential characteristic which is well defined and well known for mineral species. Therefore if we can express equation 5.1 in terms of these characteristics of a mineral substance, the total energy of the mineral substance can be calculated.

The zero state electronic energy of a diatomic mineral molecule was discussed in Chapter III and was expressed in equations 3.22 and 3.23 as e_{se}. The electronic energy in the zero state is not a function of temperature as this energy exists when the absolute temperature is zero degrees. There is a zero state electronic energy associated with every mineral molecule; we will denote this energy to be e_{seo}.

The electronic energy above the zero state; and the translational, vibrational, and rotational energies are all related to the heat capacity, C, of the substance; the heat capacity is given by;

$$C = C_e + C_t + C_v + C_r \qquad (5.2)$$

where

$C_e = \dfrac{de_{se}}{mdT}$ is the heat capacity due to the electronic energy above the ground state,

$C_t = \dfrac{de_{st}}{mdT}$ is the heat capacity due to translational energy,

$C_v = \dfrac{de_{sv}}{mdT}$ is the heat capacity due to vibrational energy,

$C_r = \dfrac{de_{sh}}{mdT}$ is the heat capacity due to rotational energy.

The energies that are a function of temperature become, when stated in terms of heat capacities:

73

$$e_{se} = m \int_0^T C_e \, dT \quad , \quad e_{st} = m \int_0^T C_t \, dT \quad ,$$

$$e_{sv} = m \int_0^T C_v \, dT \quad , \quad e_{sr} = m \int_0^T C_r \, dT \quad . \tag{5.3}$$

Substituting the mass energy expression, the zero state electronic energy, and equation 5.3 into equation 5.1, we have the following expressions for the energy of a mineral substance in terms of its essential characters;

$$e_s = mc^2 + e_{se0} + m \int_0^T [C_e + C_t + C_v + C_r] \, dT \tag{5.4}$$

or

$$e_s = mc^2 + e_{se0} + m \int_0^T C \, dT \tag{5.5}$$

Equation 5.4 applies to all the energy of a substance and includes the kinetic energy of the substance with respect to the coordinate system of the reference environment. It is convenient to select an inertially fixed rectangular coordinate system that is centered on the mineral individual under consideration. In this coordinate system, any kinetic energy of the individual substance due to motion with respect to the environment will appear as a change in environmental energy. The selection of this coordinate system allows the energy of the individual to be considered as internal energy only; the kinetic energy due to relative motion with respect to the environment now being considered as environmental energy. The mineral individual centered coordinate system does not in any way restrict the generality of the energy equations. In this coordinate system, the translational energy of the substance is zero and the energy of the substance, as given by equation 5.4 becomes;

$$e_s = mc^2 + e_{se0} + m \int_0^T [C_e + C_v + C_r] dT \quad . \qquad (5.6)$$

The mass and the zero state electronic energy, i.e., the first two terms on the right hand side of equation 5.6, represent the permanent energy of the mineral substance. This permanent energy will always be present whenever the substance exist. The permanent energy represented by the mass and zero state electronic energy is the permanent energy represented by the term e_0 in equation 3.13 of Chapter III. The integral term in equation 5.6 includes the semipermanent and transient energy internal to a substance which allows the substance to maintain an energy balance and to exchange energy with the environment. In general, the electronic energy in the integral expression of equation 5.6 is semipermanent and changes rarely in many substances. The vibrational energy is somewhat easier to change than the electronic energy and the rotational energy is relatively easy to change; it being the energy which changes with minor variations of the environmental energy. For minerals, the integral expression in equation 5.6 is equivalent to the $e_x + e_y$ terms of the general equation (3.13) for the semipermanent and transient internal energy of any substance.

5.3.2 Environmental Energy

A mineral individual's environment is usually made up of individuals of its own species, individuals of other mineral species and radiant energy. The energies of these environmental components add to form the energy environment of a given mineral individual. The energy of a given substance in the environment can be obtained from equation 5.1; the energy due to all the mineral substances in the local environment is the summation of the environmental substance's energies. This summation for substances in general is given in equation 3.14 as, $\sum_s \epsilon_s$.

The radiant energy in the environment can be specified in terms of intensity, spectral distribution, i.e., frequency distribution, direction of travel, etc. The total radiant energy in the environment is the sum of radiant energy over all frequencies

The energy in any general environment was given by equation 3.14 and is applicable to the environment of a mineral individual.

5.3.3 *Energy Exchange With The Environment*

Mineral substances are continually exchanging energy with their environment. Some of the energy exchanged with the environment is directed by the mineral. To determine the exchange energy that is directed, it is necessary to determine the forms, types, and amounts of energy being exchanged between the mineral substance and the environment.

The mechanism for changing the internal energy of a mineral substance is absorption and emission of energy across the surface of the substance. The result of this absorption and emission is an increase or decrease of the substance's energy. These changes in internal energy are a function of the method of energy transformation and the energy in the environment. We must investigate the transformation methods and environmental conditions to determine a method for calculating the exchange energy.

A mineral molecule can obtain energy from the environment by the absorption of radiant energy, and by collision with atomic particles which cause an interchange of energy with the environment. A molecule can transmit energy to the environment by these same mechanisms. The ability to absorb and emit energy under various conditions are essential characteristics of minerals. For instance, the molecules of a given species emits radiant energy only at specific wave lengths and then only under certain given energy conditions. The amount of energy that can be absorbed is related to the energy level of the substance and the amount of energy released is a function of the energy level of the substance and the amount of energy being absorbed. From quantum mechanics, it is known that absorbed energy must be related to $\frac{1}{2} h\nu$.

To quantify the energy flow through a mineral individual, it is necessary to determine the absorbed and re-emitted energy as a function of the internal energy conditions of the individual.

All minerals tend to emit energy in an attempt to reach the ground state, i.e., the lowest energy state. In general, the lowest energy state is not attained as energy from the environment is accepted by the mineral and equilibrium conditions are established. The rate of emission is a function of many things; including, the internal energy level of the substance, thermal properties of the substance, surface conditions of the substance, thermal coupling between the substance and the environment, type of material in the local environment, energy state of the environmental materials, thermal properties of the materials of the environment, etc. As stated previously, the individual can emit energy by radiation or by collision. This emitted energy results in the individual's internal energy being reduced by its changing to a lower quantum energy state. If the individual is in a vacuum, then the energy is emitted by radiation. If the individual is in an environment of other individuals which are rather widely separated, e.g., a gas, then the energy can be emitted by both radiation and collision; the energy released by collision being carried away by conduction. If the individual is in an environment of similar individuals which are in close proximity and hence mutually affect one another, such as a solid material, then the energy emitted from the individual is dependent to a large extent on the conduction of the material.

The radiant energy from a heated body can be determined from the Stefan-Boltzmann law which states that the total radiation is proportional to the fourth power of absolute temperature of the heated body. Specifically, this law states that the density of radiation or the total emissive power of a black body is proportional to the fourth power of the absolute temperature of the body, i.e.;

$$e_z = \sigma T^4. \tag{5.7}$$

77

The value of σ for a black body (perfect radiator) has been determined experimentally to be approximately 5.672×10^{-5} erg cm^{-2} degree^{-4} sec^{-1}; the emissive power having units of ergs per square centimeter per second. The emissive power of non black bodies is lower than that of a black body. A non black body will emit strongly at the same wave length at which it absorbs most readily whereas a black body will radiate and absorb at all wave lengths. The surface conditions of a non black body also effects the emissive power, e.g., a polished surface is a poor radiator. Therefore, to obtain the radiant energy of a substance the condition of its surface and its characteristic absorption and radiation frequencies must be known.

When the temperature difference between the substance and its environment is small, equation 5.7 can be simplified with only a small loss in accuracy. This simplified equation is developed as follows. Let an initial temperature (T_0) be changed by a small increment ΔT, then from equation 5.7, we have;

$$e_z = \sigma[(T_0 + \Delta T)^4 - T_0^4]$$
$$= \sigma[4T_0^3\Delta T + 6T_0^2\ \Delta T^2 + 4T_0\Delta T^3 + \Delta T^4]\ .$$

neglecting all except the first order term in ΔT, we have;

$$e_z = \sigma 4T_0^3\Delta T = C\Delta T \tag{5.8}$$

where the constants have been combined into C. Equation 5.8 was first obtained by Sir Isaac Newton and is known as the Newton cooling equation.

The quantity of heat energy transferred to the environment by conduction can be determined from the heat flow equation (Reference 5.1). These equations give the flow of heat transferred across a layer of material and the change in heat energy of a substance as a function of temperature. It has been determined experimentally that the quantity of heat transferred across a layer of material having parallel plane faces maintained at different temperature can be expressed as;

$$Q/t = KAg \tag{5.9}$$

where Q is the quantity of heat, t is time, K is the thermal conductivity of the material, A is the area of the material, and g is the temperature gradient, i.e. $g = dT/dl$, where dl is an elemental thickness of the material.

Fourier treated the general heat flow problem in his "Theorie Analytique de la Chaleur" (1822). Only the summary heat flow equation will be given herein, namely;

$$\frac{Q}{t} = KdV \left[\frac{\partial^2 T}{\partial x^2} + \frac{\partial^2 T}{\partial y^2} + \frac{\partial^2 T}{\partial z^2} \right] = K \cdot dV \cdot \nabla^2 T \qquad (5.10)$$

This equation states that the net change in heat energy per second in an elemental volume dV is equal to the thermal conductivity, K, of the material times the elemental volume times the second partial derivative of the temperature with respect to each of the three coordinates. In equation 5.10, the second partial derivaties have been denoted by ∇^2 which is sometimes called the Laplace operator.

The total emitted energy from the substance in a unit of time is obtained by adding the radiant energy, as determined from equation 5.7, to the conducted energy, as determined from equation 5.9. The loss of heat due to convection is not an important consideration for a mineral individual as the motion of fluid particles about the individual due to convection appears to be just a change in the conduction characteristics of the environment. The combination of equation 5.7 and 5.9 obtain;

$$\dot{e}_w = \sigma T^4 + KA \left(\frac{dT}{dl} \right) \qquad (5.11)$$

The energy released to the environment, at the rate given by equation 5.11, will be a miximum when the temperature of the substance is at the maximum level it can obtain and still retain its identity, i.e., not dissociate, and the temperature of the environment is at absolute zero degrees.

When the individual is in energy equilibrium with the environment, the rate of accepting energy $\dot{e}_a$ must be equal to the rate of emitting energy.

A mineral substance can be considered to have a transfer function relating the absorbed (input) energy and released (output) energy. The transfer function is the ratio of the energy output to the energy input for the mineral and gives the energy output for all types of energy inputs and internal energy states of the mineral. Values of the transfer function can be determined experimentally by measuring the energy output of a substance for given input energies, given that the internal energy states of the substance are known.

The mathematical theory required to precisely determine and describe the transfer function related to radiant energy encounters great difficulties. An approximate transfer function for mineral substances is developed below which will be adequate for our purposes.

A basic closed system showing the energy flow between a substance and the environment was shown in Figure 3-7. This figure has been redrawn as Figure 5-1 to better show the relationship between the input and output energies, and the permanent energies in the substance. The energy input rate to the substance, $\dot{e}_i$, is the local environmental energy which acts on or interacts with the substance; energy transmitted through the substance which is not influenced in any way by the substance can be ignored. Some of this energy input is rejected by the substance; this rejected energy being denoted by $\dot{e}_r$. The remaining energy input rate from the environment is accepted by the substance, this accepted energy rate is denoted by $\dot{e}_a$. By the conservation of energy principle, the rejected energy and the accepted energy must sum to the total input energy as follows;

$$e_i = e_a + e_r \qquad (5.12)$$

The transfer function H is the ratio of the output energy flow to the accepted energy flow. A schematic form of the transfer function is shown in Figure 5-2.

The accepted energy was given in Chapter III, equation 3.15 for substances in general. As indicated by equation 3.15, the accepted energy includes mechanical energy which is imparted to the substance. However due to the way the coordinate system was selected for a mineral individual, the mechanical (kinetic) energy is not accepted energy. All the remaining accepted energy appears internal to the mineral individual.

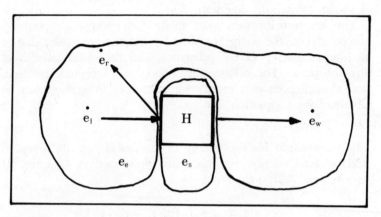

Notes:

e_e is the environmental energy.

e_s is the substance energy.

$\dot{e}_i$ is the energy rate input to the substance.

$\dot{e}_r$ is that portion of input energy rate which is rejected by the substance.

$\dot{e}_w$ is the energy rate output of the substance.

H is the total energy transfer function of the substance.

TOTAL TRANSFER FUNCTION

Figure 5-1

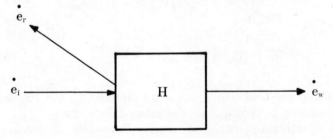

SCHEMATIC TRANSFER FUNCTION

Figure 5-2

81

The internal transfer function (H) of the mineral individual is shown pictorially in Figure 5.3.

The transfer function must relate the energy accepted by the substance, the energy released by the substance, the change in internal energy of the substance, and the characteristics of the substance. The relationship among the accepted, released, and changing internal energy for substance in general can be obtained from equation 3.16 as

$$e_w = e_a - \Delta e_s \ .$$

The relationship for the energy of any substance, its accepted and released energy, and time was developed in Chapter III as equation 3.21, namely:

$$e_s = e_{s0} + \int_0^t [\dot{e}_a(\tau) - \dot{e}_w(\tau)] d\tau \ .$$

For a mineral substance, this energy, in terms of internal conditions of the individual substance, is given by equation 5.1. Combining equations 3.21 and 5.1 obtains;

$$e_s = e_{s0} + \int_0^t [\dot{e}_a(\tau) - \dot{e}_w(\tau)] \, d\tau = e_{sm} + e_{se} + e_{st} + e_{sv} + e_{sr} \quad (5.13)$$

The accepted and the output energy of the mineral individual can be related to its specific heat and permanent energy by combining equation 3.21 and 5.6 to obtain;

$$e_s = e_{s0} + \int_0^t [\dot{e}_a(\tau) - \dot{e}_w(\tau)] \, d\tau = mc^2 + e_{se0} +$$

$$m \int_0^T [C_e + C_v + C_r] dT \quad (5.14)$$

It should be noted that equation 5.14 is valid for the coordinate system that is centered on the mineral individual.

The substance energy at time $t = 0$ consists of permanent, semipermanent, and the transient energy residing in the substance at time zero. The internal energy of a substance in terms of the permanent, semipermanent, and transient energies

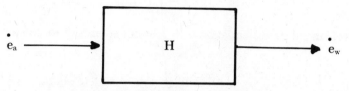

is given by equation 3.13. Using the subscript zero (0) to denote time zero, the substance energy at this time is obtained from equation 3.13 as follows:

$$e_{s0} = e_{00} + e_{x0} + e_{y0} \;. \tag{5.15}$$

As we have previously determined that the permanent energy is given by $mc^2 + e_{se0}$ for a mineral individual, we now have that,

$$e_{00} = mc^2 + e_{se0} \;. \tag{5.16}$$

Substituting equations 5.15 and 5.16 into equation 5.14 obtains;

$$e_{x0} + e_{y0} + \int_0^t [\dot{e}_a(\tau) - \dot{e}_w(\tau)]d\tau = m \int_0^T [C_e + C_v + C_r]dT \tag{5.17}$$

Equation 5.17 is the fundamental relationship among the initial energies of a mineral individual at time t_0, the energy flow into and out of the substance, and certain essential characteristics of the individual. For minerals, the internal, semipermanent and transient energies are completly determined by the temperature of the mineral at time t_0. That is;

$$e_{x0} + e_{y0} = m \int_0^{T_0} [C_e + C_v + C_r]dT \;, \tag{5.18}$$

where T_0 is the temperature of the substance at time t_0. As the right hand side of equation 5.17 can be written

$$m \int_0^{T_0} [C_e + C_v + C_r] dT + m \int_{T_0}^T [C_e + C_v + C_r] dT,$$

we can substitute equation 5.18 into equation 5.17 to obtain;

$$\int_0^t [\dot{e}_a(\tau) - \dot{e}_w(\tau)] \, d\tau = m \int_{T_0}^T [C_e + C_v + C_r] dT. \qquad (5.19)$$

Equation 5.19 expresses changes in internal energy as they relate to the energy being accepted and the energy being released by the mineral substance.

The transfer function for the mineral individual can be obtained from equation 5.19. The rate of acceptance and release of energy by the individual is obtained by differentiation of equation 5.19 with respect to time as follows;

$$\dot{e}_a - \dot{e}_w = m \frac{d}{dt} \left\{ \int_{T_0}^T [C_e + C_v + C_r] dT \right\} \qquad (5.20)$$

Let us simplify the notation in equation 5.20 by setting

$$C_i = C_e + C_v + C_r \qquad (5.21)$$

and then let us solve for the ratio of the output energy flow rate to the accepted energy flow rate as follows;

$$H = \frac{\dot{e}}{\dot{e}_a} = 1 - \left(\frac{m}{\dot{e}_a} \right) \frac{d}{dt} \left\{ \int_{T_0}^T C_i d_T \right\} \qquad (5.22)$$

Equation 5.22 is the time dependent transfer function for the energy flow through a mineral individual.

Many of the energy characteristics of a mineral substance can be obtained from the transfer function given by the preceding equations. Under equilibrium conditions, the energy flow into the substance is equal to the energy flow from the substance (i.e., $e_a = e_w$). Therefore, from equation 5.20 and 5.21 we have

84

$$m \frac{d}{dt} \left[\int_{T_0}^{T} C_i \, d_T \right] = 0$$

If $\overset{\bullet}{e}_a$ is greater than $\overset{\bullet}{e}_w$, we see from equation 5.20 that

$$m \frac{d}{dt} \left[\int_{T_0}^{T} C_i \, d_T \right]$$

must increase. As m is constant for all except the radioactive minerals,

$$\frac{d}{dt} \left[\int_{T_0}^{T} C_i \, dt \right]$$

must increase resulting in an increase of the substance's internal energy.

The internal energy of the substance, as given by equation 3.21, can be written in terms of the transfer function as follows:

$$e_s = e_{s0} + \int_0^t [\overset{\bullet}{e}_a(\tau) - H\overset{\bullet}{e}_a(\tau)] \, d\tau.$$

5.3.4 *Mineral System Energy Relationships*

A functional representation of the energy relationships for a system consisting of a mineral individual and its environment can be synthesized based on the preceding substance, environment, and exchange energy equations. A mineral-environment energy system functional diagram can be obtained by using the proper expressions for the functions given in the general system functional diagram developed in Chapter III (Figure 3-9).

A functional representation for the energy of a mineral substance is given by equation 5.6. A functional representation of the environmental energy is obtained from equation 3.14 and 3.20 as

$$e_e = \Sigma \epsilon_{s0} + \Sigma e_{z0} + \int_0^t [\overset{\bullet}{e}_w(\tau) - \overset{\bullet}{e}_a(\tau)] \, d\tau$$

where the subscript 0 indicates initial conditions. The energy release function $f_w(e_s, e_e)$ for minerals is given by equation 5.11 and is related to the energy of the substance and the environment through their temperatures, and depends on the area and conditions of the mineral's surface. The energy accepted by a mineral individual is known, from quantum mechanics, to be a function of the form $\frac{1}{2}h\nu$ where h is Planck's constant and ν is related to the characteristic frequencies of the particular mineral individual. The functional representation for a mineral individual and its environment, based on these functional representations, is shown in Figure 5-4.

5.3.5 *Directed Energy*

From the discussion of directed energy in section 3.5 of Chapter III, we know that a substance can direct certain internal and environmental energies, and energy exchanged between the environment and the substance. Directed energy equations were not developed in section 3.5 as the close relationship between the directed energy and the characteristics of a particular type substance makes it inadvisable to try developing completely generalized equations.

The considerations of mineral directed energy presented herein are based on an individual of a mineral species. Therefore, the mineral molecule will be considered without regard to the particular state the molecule is in with respect to other members of its species, e.g., the water molecule can be considered without regard to its state, namely ice, water, and vapor.

The directed energy of the substance is developed in the following dissertation as internal energy, energy flow between the substance and the environment, and environmental energy. The total directed energy of the mineral substance is obtained by summing these energies.

Directed Internal Energy

We have already determined that the directed internal energy is a subset of the internal energy of the substance, therefore the question becomes, "What portion of the substance's internal

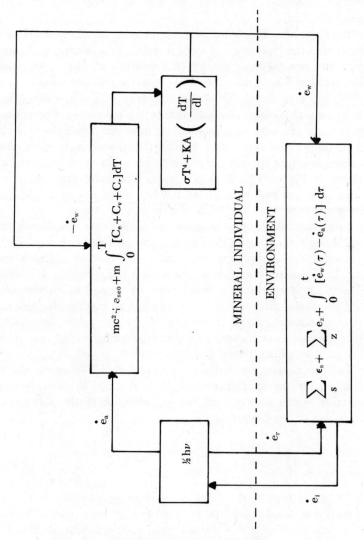

FUNCTIONAL DIAGRAM

MINERAL INDIVIDUAL-ENVIRONMENT SYSTEM

Figure 5-4

87

energy, as given by equation 5.5, can be directed by the substance?"

Based on the directed energy dissertation in Chapter III, we know that the mass energy is not directed by a substance. Therefore, the internal mass energy of a mineral substance, as given by equation 5.5, is not directed by the mineral individual.

Let us determine if the electronic energy, e_{se0}, of the substance in its ground state can be directed by the substance. The potential energy of a mineral is an absolute minimum when the mineral is in the ground state. To visualize the ground state electronic energy, consider the potential energy for a diatomic molecule as shown in Figure 3-10. It is seen from this figure that the minimum potential energy must occur when the atoms are separated by a distance of r_0 and that this minimum energy is e_{se}. The ground state electronic energy is not reduced in the formation of the molecule, during the life time of the substance, nor when the substance is destroyed. It would be extremely difficult for me to visualize the ground state electronic energy as being directed by the substance in any way. As far as I can determine, the substance does not act on, redirect, or modify the ground state electronic energy. I believe it can be safely concluded that the permanent energy of the mineral individual, i.e., $mc^2 + e_{se0}$, is not directed by the individual.

Let us examine the last term in equation 5.5 to determine if this part of the substance's energy is directed. This term is a variable which depends on the environment of the substance, the value of the expression

$$ m \int_0^T C \, dT \qquad (5.24) $$

being a function of the substance's heat capacity and temperature. From another viewpoint, this energy represents different quantum states of the substance and hence different internal arrangements or organizations to accomodate different internal energy levels. As the substance does change its internal energy configuration and hence processes or changes the energy, then by our definition of directed energy, this internal energy is di-

88

rected. To illustrate the changes in internal energy, let us consider the potential energy diagram for a diatomic molecule as shown in Figure 5-5. Assume that the diatomic molecule is initially in the ground state with energy e_{se}. Let the internal energy be increased to some higher level, say B-B in Figure 5-5, due to the vibrational energy changing from quantum state V_0 to V_1. This change in vibrational quantum state represents a change in internal energy and organization, and is considered to be a change in directed energy.

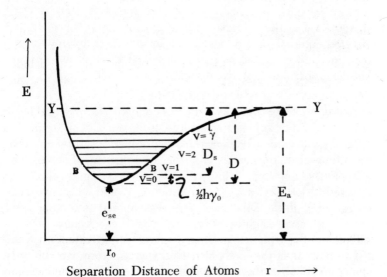

POTENTIAL ENERGY DIAGRAM OF A
DIATOMIC MOLECULE

Figure 5-5

If the internal energy were increased to the line Y-Y in Figure 5-5, then the molecule would dissociate into the two atoms and the individual would cease to exist. If we represent the difference between the ground state and the dissociation energy levels by D, then the individual has the capacity to direct an amount of energy D. The value of D is a characteristic of a mineral species and is known as the dissociation energy. The dissociation energy level is associated with a particular temperature, therefore the substance has a capability of directing a maximum internal energy of

$$[e_{ds}]_{max} = m \int_0^{T_d} C \; dT \qquad (5.25)$$

where T_d is the dissociation temperature for the particular mineral species under consideration.

Most minerals are not operating at the maximum internal energy level in their normal energy environment. The operating directed internal energy level can be obtained by integrating equation 5.25 using the normal or expected value of temperature for the upper limit of the integral.

Directed Exchange Energy

As was shown in Paragraph 5.3.3, mineral substances continually exchange energy with the environment. Let us now address the question, "How much of the exchange energy is directed?" Let us ask the question, "Would this exchange energy exist if the substance were decomposed into component parts?" Phrased slightly differently, "Is the exchange energy unique to the mineral substance under consideration?"

I submit that the exchange energy is directed by the substance. The absorption of energy from the environment and the re-emission to the environment is a function of the particular characteristics of a mineral individual. For instance, the absorption and emission of radiant energy is an essential characteristic of a particular mineral species, and the spectral nature of the absorbed and emitted radiant energy is unique to this particular mineral species. Based on these arguments, I believe that the substance acts upon the exchange energy and therefore directs this energy.

To answer the question concerning the amount of energy directed, let us consider the equilibrium (steady state) condition where the substance is in energy balance with the environment. Under these conditions, the energy accepted by the substance is equal to the energy emitted by the substance. Therefore for equilibrium conditions, there is a steady flow of energy through the substance and there is a particular internal energy condition associated with this flow of energy. As all the energy flowing through the substance is operated upon by the substance, it is, by our definition, directed energy. The amount of energy flowing through the substance can be obtained from equation 5.11. This equation gives the emitted energy as a function of the internal energy conditions of the substance, certain basic characteristics of the substance, and the energy conditions and the characteristics of the environment. As we know that for equilibrium conditions the accepted energy is equal to the emitted energy, the energy flow through the substance under these conditions can be obtained by computing the emitted energy.

The directed energy flow, which can be obtained from equation 5.11, is valid for the range of energy conditions that allow the substance to exist. However, there are two energy conditions of particular interest, namely the maximum directed energy capability and the normal or expected values of directed energy. The maximum directed exchange energy can be obtained by evaluating equation 5.11 at values of internal temperature conditions that represent the dissociation energy for the substance being considered. Referring to Figure 5-5, we see that the maximum internal energy which can be obtained by a diatomic molecule is given by E_a. There is a particular temperature of the substance associated with this energy level and there is a particular energy flow, as obtained from equation 5.11, for this particular temperature.

The normal or expected value of directed exchange energy

is that energy flowing through the substance in its normal internal energy configuration when it is in equilibrium with its normal environment. The value of this energy can be obtained by evaluating equation 5.11 using the expected energy values of the substance and the environment, and their normal configurations.

Mineral substances are either in equilibrium with their environment or they tend toward equilibrium with the environment. However, in nature, the local environment changes with time. For example, the radiant solar energy a substance receives can change very rapidly with time when a cloud comes between the sun and the substance. These environmental changes cause a change in the rate that energy is accepted from the environment and hence the substance is not in equilibrium with the environment as it is emitting energy at a rate which provided equilibrium prior to the environmental change. These time variations in directed exchange energy can be obtained by evaluating equation 5.22 under the proper set of conditions. Rearranging equation 5.22, we can evaluate the changing conditions in exchange energy from the following equation;

$$\dot{e}_w = H \dot{e}_a \qquad (5.26)$$

Directed Environmental Energy

For a mineral individual to directed energy of its environment, it must act upon, convert, or in some way change the energy of the environment. We have seen in the dissertation on exchange energy that energy coming from the environment is converted in the individual and re-emitted to the environment. However, this energy is operated upon in the substance and is not directed environmental energy. In addition, this energy has been considered once, therefore by the argument presented in Paragraph 3.5, cannot be considered again as directed energy.

Certain environmental energy impinges on the substance and is caused to change in some way at the surface of the substance, e.g., radiant energy which is reflected by the substance. I submit that this energy is directed by the mineral individual. The change in direction of a particle due to a collision with the mineral substance is another form of directed environmental energy. I consider the environmental energy which impinges upon a mineral individual and is reflected back to the environment to be directed energy.

The ability to reject energy is an essential characteristic of the substance. According to quantum mechanic theory, a substance will reject kinetic energy due to the thermal agitation, i.e., collision with the molecule, unless this energy is directly related to $h\nu$. The values of ν are known for given substances and h is Planck's constant. Quantum theory also allows the determination of the radiant energy rejection characteristics of a substance.

The rejected energy flow rate $(\dot{e}_r)$ at a given instant of time is directed energy. If the substance cannot reject energy at a sufficient rate, the accepted energy will exceed the substance's dissociation or change of state energy and the substance will expire.

The remainder of the energy in the environment is not acted upon by the mineral individual and hence is not directed. Therefore the total directed environmental energy for a mineral individual is energy rejected at the surface of the individual and is composed of radiant energy and redirected kinetic energy.

5.3.6 Total Directed Energy and Knowledge

The total directed energy can be obtained by adding the directed internal, exchange, and environmental energies. These energies can be obtained from the equations of Paragraph 5.3.5; evaluated under proper conditions. If the maximum energy capability is desired, then the equations are evaluated under conditions where the molecule is at the dissociation energy level. If the expected directed energy levels are desired, the equations are evaluated under conditions encountered in the normal substance in its normal environment.

A diagram can be synthesized to show the functional relationships for the directed energy of the mineral individual. This diagram is based on the directed energy functional relationships developed in Paragraph 5.3.5. The substance energy which is directed has been shown to be $m \int_0^T C_i dT$ (or, in expanded form, $m \int_0^T [C_e + C_v + C_r] dT$), the directed environmental energy is e_r, and all the exchange energy is directed. A functional diagram based on these directed energy relationships is shown in Figure 5-6. It should be noted that the diagram for the mineral system directed energy as shown in Figure 5-6 can be derived from the functional diagram for mineral energy systems, as shown in Figure 5-4, by deleting the energy terms which are not related to directed energy.

The knowledge of a mineral individual can be obtained from equation 4.1 by using the proper directed energy. If the directed energy is expressed in Joules then the knowledge of the mineral individual is equal to the directed energy in knowledge units.

The mineral individual has a total amount of knowledge which is determined by the maximum amount of energy it can direct. Usually the individual will not be using its total knowledge but will be operating at some lower level of knowledge associated with a lower level of directed energy. That is to say that an individual is normally not utilizing its total knowledge.

° 5.4 *Mineral Information*

Information was defined in Chapter III as the communication or transmittal of knowledge. For a mineral to have the capability of communicating or transmitting knowledge, one individual, i.e., molecule, must be able to transfer a capability of directing energy to another individual. As far as I can determine, a mineral species does not have the capability of

94

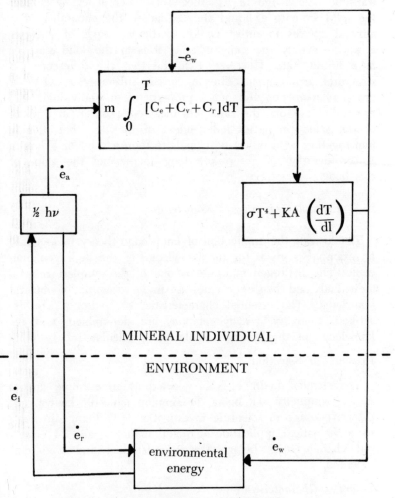

FUNCTIONAL DIAGRAM
MINERAL SYSTEM DIRECTED ENERGY

Figure 5-6

95

transmitting knowledge to other mineral species or to a member of its own species.

One could argue that a mineral substance in a solid state transmits knowledge to its "successor" when it changes from the solid state to a liquid state. That is, the capability of a mineral species to direct certain particular types of energies is approximately the same whether it is in the solid state or in a liquid state. However, I submit that the differences in structural arrangements due to various substance states is a group phenomenon and not a property of an individual, e.g., the individual has the same chemical composition and many of the same properties independent of the fact that it may join together with other individuals to form a solid or a liquid. A consideration of group knowledge is beyond the scope of this book.

°5.5 *Examples of Mineral Knowledge*

To illustrate the application of knowledge theory to minerals, an example is given for the knowledge of the hydrogen molecule. The hydrogen molecule is one of the simplest mineral individuals and hence provides a simple example of mineral knowledge. The essential characteristics of hydrogen are described, then the energy relations are determined, and the knowledge of the hydrogen molecule is calculated.

Reason For Selection

The element hydrogen was selected as an example due to its (1) simplicity — it being the simplest molecule known, (2) extensive usage in scientific investigation, (3) being amenable to mathematical application of quantum theory, and (4) essential characteristics being extensively studied and well documented.

Essential Characteristics

The hydrogen molecule (H_2) is the smallest entity which possesses the essential characteristics of hydrogen and hence is our hydrogen individual. Some of the essential characteristics of hydrogen are: atomic weight 1.0080; atomic number 1; melting point $-259.14°C$; boiling point $-252.7°C$; density 0.08988 grams/liter; specific gravity liquid 0.070 ($-252°C$); specific heat solid 0.57 calories/gram at $-260.6°C$; specific heat liquid 0.231 calories/gram at $-252°C$; dissociation energy 102.9 Kilogram calories/mole.

Hydrogen can appear in solid, liquid and gas states. From our viewpoint, these states represent various degrees of group organization among the individual (hydrogen molecule) and other like individuals in the environment. The knowledge capacity will be based on a hydrogen molecule. However, as data is more readily available on the hydrogen molecule in combination with other hydrogen molecules, this data will be used. As the performance of a single molecule is more nearly approximated by molecules in the gas state, the data on hydrogen gas is more applicable for this example. In addition, the hydrogen individual in the gas state is the more natural state in the earth environment.

Internal Knowledge: Maximum Capacity

The maximum internal knowledge capacity of a hydrogen molecule is directly related to its dissociation energy, that is, the difference between the ground state energy of the molecule and the energy level where the molecule dissociates into two hydrogen atoms. The dissociation energy of hydrogen has been determined experimentally by spectrographic means to be 102.9 thousand calories per mole (Reference 5.2). Thermal methods for obtaining the dissociation energy gives a value of 103.2 thousand calories per mole for hydrogen. To obtain the dissociation energy of a hydrogen molecule, the dissociation energy per mole must be converted to a per molecule basis. This is achieved by using Avogradro's number for the number of molecules in a gram-mole of a substance; namely 6.023×10^{23} molecules per gram-mole, and the molecular weight of hydrogen. The dissociation energy for a molecule of hydrogen is:

$$D = (102.9 \text{ K Calories/mole}) \times \left(\frac{2.016}{6.023 \times 10^{23} \text{ molecules/gram-mole}} \right)$$

$$= (3.42 \times 10^{-19} \text{ Calories}) (4.186 \text{ Joules/Calorie})$$
$$= 1.43 \times 10^{-18} \text{ Joules} \tag{5.27}$$

This energy can be directed by the hydrogen molecule, therefore the maximum internal knowledge can be obtained from equation 4.1 as follows:

$$k = e_d \text{ in knowledge units}$$
or
$$k = 1.43 \times 10^{-18} \text{ knowledge units} \tag{5.28}$$

It should be noted that this maximum internal knowledge capacity is a function only of the internal organization and structure of the hydrogen molecule and is not dependent on the environment.

Normal Internal Knowledge

The normal internal knowledge has previously been defined as the internal knowledge of the molecule under expected or normal conditions for the molecule and its environment. The internal directed energy for these conditions is obtained by integrating equation 5.24 using the normal or expected temperature of the molecule and its environment as the upper limit of the integral.

Equation 5.24 can be expanded using the component parts of the specific heat as follows:

$$e = m \int_0^T [C_e + C_t + C_v + C_r] dT. \tag{5.29}$$

Let us simplify this general equation to make it more amenable for calculating the energy of the hydrogen molecule. At equilibrium temperature conditions that can be realized in a laboratory, the electronic energy of hydrogen remains in the lowest quantum state. Therefore, the heat capacity due to electronic energy is zero, i.e., C_e is zero. When hydrogen is in a solid or liquid state, the molecules have restricted translational energy. Therefore the heat capacity due to translational energy is assumed to be zero, i.e., C_t is zero. In the gas state, hydrogen does have translational energy, however we are considering one individual gas molecule and have selected a coordinate system centered on this molecule. In this coordinate system, the molecule does not have translational energy so the heat capacity due to translational energy is zero. The selection of a coordinate system centered on the molecule was made so the translational energy could be separated form the true internal energy of the molecule. For hydrogen, equation 5.29 reduces to,

$$e = m \int_0^T C \, dT = m \int_0^T [C_v + C_r] dT \qquad (5.30)$$

The purpose of the example is to show the application of principles and not to obtain precise numerical values for the knowledge of the substances. Therefore we will make the assumption that the specific heats of solid and liquid hydrogen do not vary with temperature. This will introduce a small error but the calculation is adequate for illustration purposes. It is assumed that the specific heat of solid hydrogen is 0.57 calories per gram from $-273.16°C$ to $-259.14°C$ and the specific heat of liquid hydrogen is 0.231 calories per gram from $-259.14°C$ to $-252.7°C$. The mass of a molecule of hydrogen is determined by dividing the molecular weight of hydrogen by Avogadro's number. The molecular weight of the hydrogen molecule is 2.016 and the value for Avogrado's number is 6.023×10^{23} molecules per gram-mole. The mass of an individual molecule of hydrogen is 0.332×10^{-23} grams per molecule. For these conditions, equation 5.30 becomes;

$$e = 0.332 \times 10^{-23} \left\{ \int_{-273.16}^{-259.14} 0.57 \, dT + \int_{-259.14}^{-252.7} 0.231 \, dT + \int_{-252.7}^{T} [C_v + C_r] dT + L_i \right\}$$

where L_i is the latent heat of fusion plus the latent heat of vaporization. Therefore,

99

$$e = 0.332 \times 10^{-23} \left\{ 7.99 + 1.48 + \int_{-252.7}^{T} [C_v + C_r] \, dT + 14 + 108 \right\}$$

where the heat of fusion is 14 calories/gram and the heat of vaporization is 108 calories/gram. This equation becomes

$$e = 0.332 \times 10^{-23} \int_{-252.7}^{T} [C_v + C_r] dT + 43.65 \times 10^{-23} \text{ Calories} \quad (5.31)$$

The specifiic heat for hydrogen gas at constant volume is given in Figure 5-7. As indicated by equation 5.30, we are interested only in the specific heat due to rotation and vibration of the hydrogen molecule. Therefore, we determine the value of

$$\int_{-252.7}^{T} [C_v + C_r] dT$$

by obtaining the area between a curve of C_v and a $(3/2)R$ line from 20.40°K to the temperature of interest (T). Let us assume the normal energy of hydrogen to be approximately the ambient temperature of the earth environment (290°K). We see from Figure 5-7 that vibrational energy is not involved in the temperature range up to 290°K. Therefore, equation 5.31 becomes,

$$e = 0.332 \times 10^{-23} \int_{-252.7}^{16.84} C_r \, dT + 43.65 \times 10^{-23}$$

Let us compute the integral graphically. A curve of C for the temperature range from 50°K to 275°K is given in Figure 5-8. The area between curve A and B over this temperature interval is the internal energy due to rotation of the molecule in calories per mol. This energy is 214 calories per mol. Curve B has approximately a constant value of 5 calories per mol per degree between 275°K and 290°K. Another 30 calories per mol must be added to include this temperature range. The

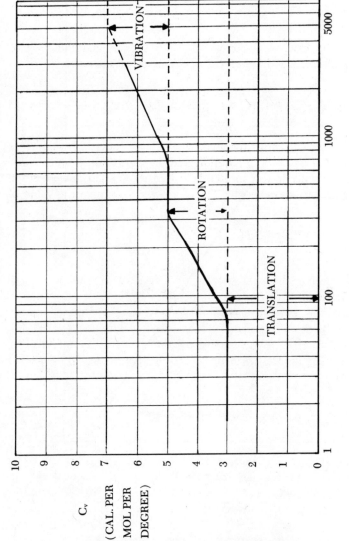

SPECIFIC HEAT OF HYDROGEN

Figure 5-7

101

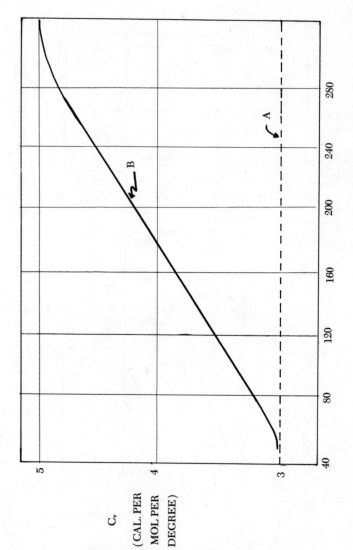

SPECIFIC HEAT OF HYDROGEN
(LOW TEMPERATURES)

Figure 5-8

resultant energy due to rotation is 244 calories per mol or 122 calories per gram. The value of the directed internal energy under normal conditions is,

$$e_{ds} = (0.332 \times 10^{-23})\ (122) + 43.65 \times 10^{-23} \text{ calories,}$$

which equals 3.5×10^{-21} Joules.

The normal internal knowledge, i.e., knowledge utilized by the hydrogen individual in an ordinary environment, is;

$$k = 3.5 \times 10^{-21} \text{ knowledge units.} \tag{5.32}$$

These calculated values are not exact due to the various assumptions used in the calculations. Based on this calculation of normal internal knowledge, the hydrogen individual is normally operating at a knowledge level which is very small compared to its total internal knowledge capability.

Exchange Knowledge: *Maximum Capacity*

The exchange knowledge is dependent on the characteristics of the substance and the environment to such an extent that these characteristics must be specified in detail in order to obtain values of exchange knowledge. As the purpose of this example is to illustrate principles rather than to obtain precise values for the knowledge of hydrogen, certain assumptions are made to simplify the calculations and to better illustrate the principles.

The maximum exchange energy occurs when the internal energy of the molecule is equal to the dissociation energy. As shown in Paragraph 5.33, the exchange energy can be obtained by determining the emitted energy. The maximum exchange energy is obtained by evaluating equation 5.11 for maximum temperature conditions. The maximum temperature can be approximated from the dissociation energy by making certain simplifying assumptions. Let us make the assumptions of classical theory that the energy of a molecule is equally distributed among its various degrees of freedom and that the energy per degree of freedom is expressed by $e = \frac{1}{2}kT$ where k

103

is "Boltzmann's constant" and is equal to 1.38×10^{-16} erg deg^{-1}, and T is the absolute temperature. The dissociation energy is given by equation 5.27 as 1.43×10^{-18} Joules, i.e., 1.43×10^{-11} ergs. A diatomic molecule, such as hydrogen, has seven degrees of freedom (Reference 5.3), therefore the temperature for hydrogen at the dissociation energy can be obtained as follows;

$$e = 7/2 \ kT \text{ and,}$$

$$T = (2/7)(e/k) = \left\{ \frac{(2)(1.43 \times 10^{-11})}{(7)(1.38 \times 10^{-16})} \right\} = 3.14 \times 10^{4} \text{ deg K.}$$

The maximum radiant energy can be obtained by evaluating equation 5.7 at the maximum temperature, i.e.,

$$e_z = (5.672 \times 10^{-5} \text{ ergs cm}^{-2}\text{deg}^{-4}\text{sec}^{-1})(3.14 \times 10^{4}\text{deg})^{4}$$
$$= 5.5 \times 10^{13} \text{ ergs cm}^{-2}\text{sec}^{-1}.$$

To obtain the energy radiated from the hydrogen molecule, the effective radiating area must be obtained. The molecule does not have a radiating surface in the sense normally used in determining radiation from large bodies; however, it has an effective or equivalent radiating surface area. For purpose of illustration, it is assumed that the effective radiating area is equivalent to the area of a sphere having a diameter of 1.2×10^{-8} cm; this diameter is obtained from classical theory (Reference 5.4). The effective radiating area of the hydrogen molecule, under this assumption, is;

$$A = \pi D^{2} = \pi (1.20 \times 10^{-8})^{2} = 4.52 \times 10^{-16} \text{ cm}^{2}.$$

The maximum radiated energy for the hydrogen molecule under these assumptions is;

$$e_z = (5.5 \times 10^{13} \text{ ergs cm}^{-2} \text{ sec}^{-1})(4.52 \times 10^{-16} \text{ cm}^{2})$$
$$= 2.5 \times 10^{-9} \text{ Joules/sec .} \tag{5.33}$$

An insight into the energy released from the hydrogen molecule by conduction can be obtained by making certain assumptions about the characteristics and the energy conditions of the environment. Let us assume that the environment consists of other hydrogen molecules, hence we are dealing with a hydrogen gas environment. Also assume that a maximum energy flow rate exists due to the temperature of the environment being zero degrees Kelvin at a distance of one centimeter from the hydrogen molecule of interest. This condition would be extremely unlikely in any physical system, but does represent a maximum energy flow. The energy flow can be obtained from equation 5.9 as follows. The value for the thermal conductivity (K) of hydrogen gas is 3.63×10^{-4} calories sec^{-1} cm^{-2} for a thermal gradient of $1°C$ per cm (Reference 5.5). The area is assumed to be the same as that used for the radiation calculation. The energy flow due to conduction, under the given assumptions, is;

$$Q/t = KAg = (3.63 \times 10^{-4}) \ (4.52 \times 10^{-16}) \ (2.96 \times 10^{4})$$

$$= 4.85 \times 10^{-15} \text{ calories/sec,}$$

$$\text{or} \quad Q/t = 2.02 \times 10^{-14} \text{ Joules/sec.} \tag{5.34}$$

The total emitted energy is obtained by adding equations 5.33 and 5.34; however, it is seen that the radiant energy is the dominant term so that the emitted energy is equal to the radiant energy given by equation 5.33. One of the major uncertainties in the calculation of the radiant energy is due to the assumed effective radiating area. This area also appears in the calculation of the conducted energy, therefore the ratio of the radiant to the conducted energy should be representative of the relative contribution of these energies to the total energy. In general, one would expect that at high temperatures the radiant energy determines the energy transfer.

The total maximum energy flow for the hydrogen individual of our example is 2.5×10^{-9} Joules/sec. To obtain the knowledge associated with this energy flow, we must obtain the energy which has flowed for some period of time, i.e.,

$$e_w = \int_{t_1}^{t_2} (2.5 \times 10^{-9}) dt,$$

or

$$e_w = (2.5 \times 10^{-9})t \Big|_{t_1}^{t_2} \ .$$

Recognizng the changes of knowledge with time where these changes are some times rapid, it will be convenient to select the basic unit of time as the time interval, i.e. the second. Therefore for purposes of obtaining the individual's knowledge, the emitted energy will be obtained over a one second interval. For our example, we have that the directed exchange energy is 2.5×10^{-9} Joules which results in a maximum exchange knowledge of 2.5×10^{-9} knowledge units.

Normal Exchange Knowledge

The knowledge level associated with the normal exchange energy is obtained by evaluating the exchange knowledge and directed exchange energy equation under normal conditions for the hydrogen molecule and its environment. The method for evaluating the normal exchange energy is the same as that for the maximum exchange energy, i.e., the energy emitted to the environment is used to calculate the exchange energy. Once the emitted energy is determined, then equilibrium conditions are assumed which implies that the environment is supplying energy to the hydrogen molecule at the same rate the molecule is emitting energy.

Calculation of the exchange energy of the hydrogen molecule under normal conditions is performed assuming the normal temperature to be approximately the same as the average earth temperature; namely $290°K$. It is also assumed that the radiating area of the hydrogen molecule is the same as that used in the determination of the maximum exchange energy, i.e., 4.52×10^{-16} cm^2, and that the Stefan-Boltzmann constant (σ) is valid for the hydrogen molecule. Under these assumptions, the normal emitted radiant energy is;

$$e_z = \sigma T^4 = (5.672 \times 10^{-5}) \ (290)^4 \ (4.52 \times 10^{-16})$$
$$= 1.82 \times 10^{-10} \text{ ergs/sec. or } 1.82 \times 10^{-17} \text{ Joules/sec.}$$

The energy emitted from the hydrogen molecule for the normal temperature due to conduction can be calculated based on the same assumptions as those used for determining the maximum exchange knowledge. Under these assumptions, the emitted energy due to conduction into a hydrogen gas environment is;

$$Q/t = KA \left(\frac{dT}{dl} \right) = (3.63 \times 10^{-4}) \ (4.52 \times 10^{-16}) \ (290)$$

$$= 4.75 \times 10^{-17} \text{ calories/sec.}$$

or $Q/t = (4.75 \times 10^{-17} \text{ cal/sec}) \ (4.186 \text{ Joules/cal})$
$$= 19.8 \times 10^{-17} \text{ Joules/sec.}$$

The total emitted energy flowing from the hydrogen molecule is the sum of the radiant and conduction energies, namely;

$$\dot{e}_w = e_z + Q/t = 1.82 \times 10^{-17} \text{ Joules/sec} + 1.98 \times 10^{-16} \text{ Joules/sec}$$
$$= 2.16 \times 10^{-16} \text{ Joules/sec.}$$

The directed exchange energy in a one second time interval is;

$$e_w = \int_t^{t+1} 2.16 \times 10^{-16} \ dt \ = 2.16 \times 10^{-16} \text{ Joules.}$$

The knowledge associated with this directed energy is 2.16×10^{-16} knowledge units.

Environmental Knowledge

The environmental knowledge of a mineral individual was stated in Paragraph 5.3.5 to be a function of the environmental energy that is rejected by the mineral individual. The rate of energy rejection by the individual is a direct function of the magnitude and form of the energy impinging on the individual and the rejection characteristics of the individual. Therefore, the rejected energy and hence the knowledge associated with this energy cannot be determined until the rejection characteristics of the substance are completely specified.

When these properties are specified, then the rejected energy flow rate can be determined, it being the energy that is neither absorbed by the individual nor transmitted through the individual. Once the rate of energy rejection has been determined, the knowledge associated with the rejected energy can be calculated.

Due to the sensitivity of rejected energy to the surface conditions of the substance and to environmental energy conditions, any calculation of the normal directed energy would be very restrictive and, in fact, may be misleading if extrapolated to general considerations. Therefore, calculations are not performed but instead a general method of solution is given.

The required characteristics of the environment which must be determined are the amplitude and the frequency distribution of all radiant energy impinging on the hydrogen molecule, and all the energy content of the particles in the environment that collide with the molecule. The required characteristics of the hydrogen molecule which must be determined are the allowable quantum states, so that the energy absorption and rejection characteristics can be determined. When these properties have been determined, the amount of energy rejected under these conditions can be calculated. The environmental knowledge can be determined from this directed energy.

Total Knowledge of Hydrogen

The knowledge of hydrogen for maximum and for normal conditions can be obtained by addition of the component knowledge values developed above; addition of the knowledge components being in accord with theorem I.

Let us first consider the knowledge required for a hydrogen molecule to just survive under maximum energy conditions. The knowledge associated with this condition is the sum of the maximum internal knowledge, the maximum exchange knowledge, and the maximum environmental knowledge (k_e). From the values developed in the preceding paragraphs, we have:

$$k_{max} = 1.43 \times 10^{-18} + 2.5 \times 10^{-9} + k_e \text{ knowledge units.}$$

As we have not determined the value of the molecule's knowledge of the environment (k_e), let us consider only the internal and the exchange knowledge. This obtains a value of 2.5×10^{-9} knowledge units which represents the total internal and exchange knowledge of the molecule.

Let us now consider the normal knowledge. This knowledge is the sum of the internal, exchange, and environmental knowledge associated with the "normal" environment. Considering only the internal and exchange knowledge as calculated in the preceding paragraphs, we have;

$$k_n = 3.5 \times 10^{-21} + 2.16 \times 10^{-16}$$
$$= 2.16 \times 10^{-16} \text{ knowledge units.}$$

It is again noted that the purpose of the example is to illustrate the application of knowledge theory to a mineral individual and not to obtain numerical values for a particular substance. It should also be noted that the example gives a steady state solution. If the short time variations are desired, the transfer functions could be used for these short term knowledge calculations. It should be further noted that the knowledge level utilized by the hydrogen molecule is very small compared to its total knowledge.

Chapter VI

PLANT KNOWLEDGE

6.0 Introduction

In this chapter, the principles of knowledge are applied to the plant kingdom. Certain principles of biology and botany are reviewed, the classification and essential characteristics of plants are given, and the equations for energy and knowledge as they apply to plants are developed. Examples are given to demonstrate the applicability of the knowledge equation for plants.

It is not my intent to develop a complete and exhaustive set of equations for the determination of plant knowledge, but to develop general equations which will indicate the applicability of knowledge theory to plants.

6.1 Characteristics of Plants

The most important characteristic of a plant is life. All plants have life, this characteristic being the major consideration in differentiating plants from minerals. Therefore, it is essential to define a living organism. The necessary and sufficient condition for a substance to be recognized as a living organism is that it be a discrete mass of matter with a definite structure or boundary, undergoing continual interchange of material with its environment without manifest alteration of basic characteristics over short periods of time, and originating by some process of division or fractionation from one or two pre-existing substances of the same kind.

The continual exchange of material with the environment may be called the metabolic criterion and the origin from pre-existing substances may be called the reproductive criterion.

Certain inanimate systems satisfy the metabolic criterion. An often cited example is a steady flame, which has a definite boundary, may remain unchanged for an appreciable period of time and is continually accepting oxygen from the environment and producing carbon dioxide and water.

If we consider radiant energy to be corpuscular, i.e., material in the form of a photon, then all inanimate systems can meet the metabolic criterion as they accept and give off material in the form of photons. The reproduction criterion is necessary to distinguish living substances from mineral substances and inanimate systems which have not been observed to arise from division or fragmetation of pre-existing members of the same class. Application of the reproduction criterion implies the ability to differentiate classes of organisms based on form, behavior, etc. The discipline of organism classification based on their distinguishing characteristics is the taxonomy branch of biology.

In rare cases, difficulties may arise in applying the life criterion to living organisms. Satisfaction of the metabolic criterion may be suspended in the case of latent or suspended animation; e.g., a few small invertebrate animals exhibit normal life functions after having been exposed to temperatures little above absolute zero ($-273\,^\circ$C). These cases could be taken care of by stating the conditions under which the definition applies. A second difficulty is possibly introduced by the supposed mode of origin of certain double stars. If cosmic matter continually fell into a star, it would grow in mass. However, there is a critical size above which radiation pressure ceases to be counter-balanced by gravitation and the star becomes unstable and breaks into two or more parts. Under these circumstances, a star could fall within the definition of a living organism except that the mode of origin of the new pair by fission must be an exceptional event and there would be no evidence that the initial parent star arose in any comparable way.

The above definition of a living organism is probably the most satisfactory one at this point in time. Actually, from the earliest time, philosophers have attempted to define life without one completely satisfactory definition having been advanced. Today, the difficulties of their task can be appreciated because it becomes increasingly evident that there is no clear line of demarcation between the living and the nonliving. Nevertheless, as Claude Bernard indicated in his essay on the "Phenomena of Life", there are a number of properties of living matter which, taken collectively, serve as a rough and ready means of differentiating life from relatively inert systems. These are:

- Assimilation and respiration
- Reproduction
- Growth and development
- Movement
- Secretion and excretion.

Considered singly, no one of these is in itself characteristic of living matter alone, but as yet, no system that could be considered as a non-living one has been found to exhibit all of these properties together. Let us now consider the major characteristics of plants in more detail.

Assimilation and Respiration

The changing of food into living substance is called assimilation. All plants have the capability to assimilate material and convert the material into energy forms required for the plant to live. Green plants have the capability of synthesizing complex organic substances from carbon dioxide, water and simple inorganic salt such as sulphates, nitrates and phosphates. Nongreen plants break down food into forms of energy the plant can use.

The term respiration is used in biology and bio-chemistry to describe the oxidation of material to support the life processes.

The sum total of the activities, maintenance, repair and growth in living organism is known as metabolism. The mechanisms and processes of metabolism are essential characteristics of plants and certain parts of the process may be unique to a particular species. The metabolic machinery by which chemical changes are brought about consists of enzymes. Essentially an enzyme is an organic catalyst for a specific reaction.

113

Reproduction

The ability to reproduce is an essential characteristic of all plants. Everything that lives sooner or later dies, as opposed to inanimate objects which may never die. In Chapter V we stated that minerals in equilibrium with the environment do not die, a change in the environment being required before the mineral will die, i.e., change state. Plants do not exhibit this characteristic. They will die sooner or later even though the environment remains constant. However, a plant species continues to live through the reproduction process. The reproduction process is important to the theory of knowledge as certain information must be transmitted from one generation to another. Genetics is the study of methods for transmitting basic organizational knowledge from one generation to another.

Growth and Development

Growth, as used herein, is defined in the biological sense. That is, growth takes place through the activity of protoplasm; it can occur in no other way. As such, growth is essentially an irreversible process and involves more than just an increase in size or in weight. The above definition of growth precludes increases in weight due to absorption of water being considered as growth.

Growth and development are essential characteristics of plants. All plants start from one cell during each generation; therefore, growth is essential to plants, especially the multicellular plants. The mass of a plant varies as a function of the growth process. This is in contrast to the mineral kingdom where the mass of a substance is constant and can be used as an indicator of the substance's energy.

The living matter of a substance has been named protoplasm by the biologist and most biologists believe that protoplasm owes its living nature to its organization rather than to the possession of some particular vital element (Reference 6.1). The mass of a plant should be a good indication of its energy; however, it is probably not as important as for mineral substances. The method of growth is an important characteristic of plants.

114

Movement

Plants have movement due to growth and in some cases in response to stimuli from the environment. Little is known, at the present time, of the factors determining the growth movements of plants beyond Loeb's having shown by his research on regeneration in Bryophyllum that chemical factors probably play a part in the directional growth of shoots and roots (Reference 6.2).

Secretion and Excretion

Plants excrete certain material, such as carbon dioxide, into the soil. The process by which plants excrete materials has been scarcely investigated (Reference 6.3). The excretion of material from a plant is an important characteristic in determining the flow of energy across the interface between the plant and the environment.

6.2 Nomenclature and Classification of Plants

To determine the knowledge-energy relationship for a given plant species, it is necessary to be able to distinguish between the various species, or classes, of plants. The classification of plants can be traced to the ancient Greeks. During the ancient Greek period and during the middle ages, plants were classified mainly by such characteristics as structure, growth habits, etc. The presently accepted method is based mainly on reproductive structures and behavior with the vegetative characteristics being of secondary importance. This method has gained favor because the reproductive characteristics are less likely to be influenced by environmental factors than the vegetable characteristics.

6.2.1 Plant Classification

A complete arrangement of the major groups of plants or of all plants into a unified scheme is called a classification system. General classification grouping have been established as follows:

Species: The species is the basic unit of organism classification. A species is a kind of living organism (e.g. a dog, a white oak, a sugar maple, etc.). A species may be defined technically as the usually smallest unit in the classification system; it is a group of individuals of the same ancestry of similiar structure and behavior, and of stability in nature; that is, the members of a species retain their characteristic features through many generations under natural conditions. In many groups of plants, species are sharply delimited; in other groups, there are no sharp lines between species because of intermediate forms. Sometimes there are different types (varieties) of organisms within a species; for example, the various kinds of dogs are all varieties of the dog species; such varieties do not maintain themselves in nature, but are maintained artificially by man.

Genera: A genus is a collection of closely related species. For example, the oak genus contains the white, chestnut, bur, live, scarlet and bear oak species. All have certain common major characteristics, but differ somewhat in minor ways.

Families: A family is a group of closely related genera. For example, the oak family contains the chestnut genus (Castanea), the oak genus (Quercus), etc. These genera have certain traits in common which show them to be related; however, there are certain large differences among them.

Orders: An order is a group of closely related families which have certain traits in common but which differ in certain respects. The oak order is named the Fagales (birch order).

Classes: A class is a group of related orders having similar features. The oak is in the dicotyledoneae class (plants with two seed leaves).

Phyla: A phylum is a group of related classes. The oak is in the Spermatophyta phylum (seed plants).

6.2.2. *Essential Plant Characteristics*

The classification system described in Paragraph 6.2.1, is based on certain similarities and differences in reproduction and structural considerations. These characteristics are important for the identification and classification of plants but are not the most essential elements for determining plant knowledge-energy relationships.

The essential characteristics for the determination of plant knowledge relate to (1) mass of the plant, (2) the temperature of the plant, (3) metabolism, (4) method of energy transfer between the plant and the environment, (5) methods of extracting energy from the environment, (6) work done on the environment, (7) structural organization of the plant, and (8) method of transferring knowledge from one substance to another. Modification of the knowledge transferred from one generation to another in a given species is also an important consideration in this theory of knowledge.

6.3   Knowledge of Plants

In plants, as in minerals, we are interested in determining the knowledge and energy relationships for the smallest amount of the substance which still possesses the essential characteristics of that substance. For plants, the smallest organism is an individual of a given species. The size of plant individuals vary from microscopic one cell plant species to large organisms such as the redwood and giant sequoia trees.

A single living plant organism is the smallest unit which can exist by itself and retain all the properties of the original substance. This definition is for plants as the molecule is for mineral substances.

6.3.1   Individual Plant Energy

To obtain the knowledge of an individual plant, it is necessary to determine the energy of the individual and the subset of this energy that is directed by the individual. Mathematical expressions for an individual's energy can be obtained by adapting the general expression for a substance's energy, as given in Chapter III equation 3.12, to a form suitable for plants. Equation 3.12 is completely general and therefore applies to

117

an individual plant, given that the terms of the equations are stated in proper relationship to the characteristics of the plant and all the energy forms of the plant are considered. Equation 3.12 gives the energy of a substance as the sum of the energy types which constitute the substance. A plant's energy can be considered in terms of the constituent parts of the plant. The general consensus of opinion is that the living nature of protoplasm is due to organization rather than to any one vital element. Therefore, the internal energy content of a plant should be the sum of the energy of all its constituent parts plus the energy of formation for these parts. The characteristics and types of the elements which constitute a plant are either known or can be determined. Therefore, the energy of the constituent parts could be calculated by determining the energy level of each molecule in the substance by summing over all elements (molecules) that make up the substance. The energy of formation must be added to this sum to obtain the total plant energy. The equation for the energy of a plant, as determined from the constituent parts, becomes:

$$e_s = \sum_i \sum_j e_{sij} \tag{6.1}$$

where the subscript i denotes the ith molecule of the plant and j the jth energy form.

The energy of an individual molecule of a mineral is given by equation 5.4 of Chapter V. The energy of the plant due to the individual molecules of the plant is the summation of these individual energies as obtained from equation 5.4. This energy is given as;

$$\sum_i \left\{ m_i c^2 + e_{se0i} + m_i \int_0^T (C_{ei} + C_{ti} + C_{vi} + C_{ri}) dT \right\} \tag{6.2}$$

The mass of the individual molecules must sum to the total mass of the plant, therefore equation 6.2 can be written as;

$$mc^2 + \sum_i \left\{ e_{se0i} + m_i \int_0^T (C_{ei} + C_{ti} + C_{vi} + C_{ri}) dT \right\} \tag{6.3}$$

118

or

$$mc^2 + \sum_i \left\{ e_{se0i} + m_i \int_0^T c_i \, dT \right\} \qquad (6.4)$$

The energy of the plant given by equation 6.4 includes the mass, ground state electronic, and the heat energies. However, equation 6.4 does not account for all the energies of a plant. The additional energies of the plant are due to the mechanical motion of certain molecules of the plant with respect to the general coordinates of the plant, and to the energy of protoplasm formation. The mechanical motion of certain molecules with respect to most of• the plant molecules is due to such factors as capillary action, different concentrations of solutions caused by metabolic process, transpiration, etc. The energy of formation is esentially stored in the plant in the form of chemical energy which can be recovered if the plant constituents were dissociated into simpler forms of matter.

If a coordinate system is selected which is centered on the plant, then the majority of the molecules which constitute the plant will be stationary with respect to this coordinate system. There will be certain short term movements due to thermal agitation, etc., but on a long term basis, they can be considered to be stationary with respect to the plant centered coordinate system. However, other molecules will have motion with respect to this coordinate system, e.g., the metabolic process causes different concentrations of materials within the plant which results in a flow of metabolic by products out of the plant. Another example of this motion is the flow of sap in some of the more highly developed plants, i.e., those with veins. Let M_j be the miscellaneous energy of the plant due to metabolism, capillary action, etc.; then the miscellaneous energy internal to the plant is given by:

$$\sum_j M_j , \qquad (6.5)$$

where the subscript j indicates the energy associated with a particular phenomonon, e.g. the mechanical energy due to capillary action. The miscellaneous energy must be evaluated for the particular plant species under consideration as the forms of energy vary from species to species.

When a plant assimilates food into protoplasm, it in essence stores chemical energy. In addition, when green plants synthesize complex organic substances from inorganic material and solar energy, they increase their potential chemical energy. In these processes, energy is supplied from some external source, such as solar energy, to cause the formation of the complex organic materials. As these resulting complex materials are internal to the plant, their chemical energies of formation are considered to be stored as potential internal energy of the plant. Indeed, if these materials were to be dissociated through oxidation, the formation energies would be released. During the growth of a plant, protoplasm is formed. Energy is expended in the formation of the protoplasm which can be compared to the formation energies of mineral molecules and compounds. This formation energy process continues as long as the plant grows. The formation energy of a plant represents the degree of organization of the plant. For example, the formation energy of a seedling plant is smaller than the formation energy of a mature plant. Likewise, the organization of a seedling is smaller than that of a mature plant.

Although the 'organizational energy, i.e., formation energy, of plants is an important aspect of a plants energy, it is not treated in depth herein due to the complexity of the problem and a general lack of information in this area of investigation. However, a crude indication of the organizational energy. is presented below. If the energy of formation for a particular type of living material is e_f in energy units per unit mass of material, and there are m units of mass, then the formation energy of a certain amount of the material is:

$$e = e_{fk} m_k , \qquad (6.6)$$

where the subscript k indicates the kth type of material. The total energy of formation e_f is then summation of all the k materials which make up the plant, i.e.,

$$e_t = \sum_k e_{fk} m_k . \qquad (6.7)$$

120

This equation can be combined with equations 6.4 and 6.5 to obtain;

$$e_s = mc^2 + \sum_i \left(e_{seoi} + m_i \int_0^T C_i \ dT \right) + \sum_j M_j + \sum_k e_{fk} m_k \ . \quad (6.8)$$

At any time in its life, a plant is composed of a certain mass made up of various living materials. If these materials were burned, e.g., by the catabolism process, a certain amount of energy would be released. The burning of the material, and the subsequent release of energy is somewhat equivalent to the energy of dissociation of minerals. If it is assumed that the energy released in the burning process is the energy of dissociation of the living material and that it also represents the energy required to form the living material from raw material, then this energy is an indication of the energy of formation, i.e. the organizational energy.

The amount of energy released by the metabolic burning of materials such as carbohydrates, proteins, and certain fats have been experimentally determined. With these values and the composition of the plant, a crude indication of the organizational energy can be obtain from equation 6.7.

Plants have the capability of storing foodstuff internal to their structure which can be converted to heat and mechanical energy under the proper set of conditions. The amount of this stored potential energy is a function of the amount of foodstuff, the type of foodstuff stored, and the efficiency of the plant in converting a specific type of foodstuff into a usable form of energy. Let us assume that a plant in a particular stage of development has a mass m_0 which is associated with the basic structure of the plant. That is to say, m_0 is the mass of the plant when it does not contain stored foodstuffs. Let us also assume that the plant in this given stage of development has a stored mass of foodstuff m_{fs} and that $m_0 + m_{fs}$ is equal to the total mass (m) of the plant. Let us further assume that the plant can metabolize the stored foodstuff in such a way that the energy released from the foodstuff is;

$$e = Fm_{Fs} \qquad (6.9)$$

where F is a property of the plant and the type of foodstuff being metabolized. Equation 6.9 is the potential energy stored by the plant in the form of foodstuff. When the potential energy of the plant due to stored foodstuff is converted by metabolism, the predominant energy resulting from the process is in the form of heat.

The metabolism of internally stored foodstuff is carried out in approximately the same way in all plants, depending on certain thermal and environmental conditions. For example, the chemical equation for the reduction of a given foodstuff is similar in all plants and the heat of reaction is the same. Therefore, by knowing the chemical process, and the amount and type of stored foodstuff, the amount of energy released can be determined and hence the amount of stored potential energy. The rate of metabolizing the stored energy is governed by temperature, rate and method of disposing of metabolism byproducts, etc.

As the stored energy is an important consideration, it is desirable to break it out separately in equation 6.8. The equation becoming, upon combining equations 6.8 and 6.9;

$$e_s = mc^2 + \sum_i \left(e_{seoi} + m_i \int_0^T C_i dT \right) + \sum_j M_j + \sum_k e_{fk} m_{0k} + F m_{Fs}.$$

$$(6.10)$$

The energy of a plant, as given by this equation, is for one particular time in the life of the plant. For example, the equation will be different at an early time in the growth of a plant than when the plant is mature.

6.3.2 *Exchange Energy*

The internal energy of a plant can be maintained only by an exchange of energy with the environment. This continual exchange of energy permits the plant to be in equilibrium, i.e., energy balance, with its environment. To determine the amount of the exchange energy that is directed, the total amount of exchange energy must be determined. Both the total amount of energy exchanged with the environment and the short term changes in exchange energy are of interest.

The procedure for determining the total exchange energy for plants is the same as that given in Chapter V for minerals; namely, the energy flowing from the individual to the environment is determined, and as the individual is in equilibrium with the environment, it must accept energy from the environment at the same rate it releases energy to the environment. As a plant is a particular organization of minerals, it should exhibit many basic energy properties of minerals. Indeed one would expect the radiant and the conduction energy released from the plant to the environment to have the same form as that for minerals, i.e.:

$$\sigma T^4 + KA \left(\frac{dT}{dl} \right)$$

where the constants σ, K, and A are the radiation constant, the coefficient of conduction, and the superficial area of the plant respectively.

In addition to the energy exchange due to radiation and conduction, a plant exchanges energy with the environment through the metabolic process. The rate at which the metabolic process liberates heat energy and releases materials into the environment is a function of the temperature of the plant and the environment. In general, the metabolic process of plants stops below zero degrees centigrade, increases as the temperature increases above zero to some maximum value, which is usually at approximately the mean value of the local environmental temperature, and then decreases until a temperature is reached which kills the plant, hence stopping the metabolic process. The metabolic rate is also a function of the plant species. Although the basic chemical reaction for the metabolic process is similar in all plants, individual differences, such as cell permeability to various solutions, can occur among plant species.

The basic summary chemical equation for plant catabolism (respiration) is;

$$C_6H_{12}O_6 + 6O_2 \longrightarrow 6CO_2 + 6H_2O + \text{energy} \qquad (6.11)$$

(see Reference 6.4). The carbon dioxide and the water resulting from this catabolic process passes to the environment in the form of matter. The free energy resulting from the process can be in the form of heat, it can furnish energy for other chemical processes, or it can perform mechanical work; the most prevalent form is heat. Therefore, the plant can transmit mass energy, heat energy, and mechanical energy to the environment. One would expect the rate of transfer of energy to the environment to be a function of the superficial area of the plant. Indeed it has been adequately demonstrated that the acceptance of energy in the metabolism process of photosynthesis is a direct function of the leaf surface area (Reference 6.5) and it has been verified that the catabolism process in animals is a function of the superficial area of the animal (Reference 6.6).

The rate at which a mature plant releases energy to the environment due to the metabolism process can be determined from equation 6.11 and the metabolic rate. The rate of mass transferred to the environment ($\dot{m}_T$) is equal to the mass ($\dot{m}_p$) of carbon dioxide and water resulting from the catabolism of one $C_6H_{12}O_6$ molecule times the catabolism rate in molecules of $C_6H_{12}O_6$ per second ($\dot{\beta}$). The rate of free energy (e_F) generation is equal to the energy liberated by the catabolism of one molecule of food times the catabolism rate in molecules of food per second ($\dot{\beta}$). Therefore, the rate of mass transfer to the environment is:

$$\dot{m}_T = m_p \dot{\beta} \qquad (6.12)$$

and the energy transferred due to catabolism is;

$$\dot{e}_{wc} = \dot{\beta} \left(m_p c^2 + \gamma_t e_F \right) \qquad (6.13)$$

where γ_t is that fractional part of the energy freed in the catabolism process which is transferred to the environment. The remaining energy freed during the catabolism process is used to carry on the internal processes such as growth, secondary metabolic processes, etc.

124

The energy transferred to the environment from the substance is obtained by combining the energies due to radiation, conduction, and catabolism. If it is assumed that the catabolism process does not materially affect the temperature of the plant, then the free energy of catabolism can be considered independently of the radiation and conduction energy thus allowing equation 6.13 to be added to the equations for the radiation and conduction energies. The resulting equation for the transmitted energy rate is:

$$e_w^{\bullet} = \sigma T^4 + KA \left(\frac{dT}{dl} \right) + \dot{\beta}(m_p c^2 + \gamma_t e_F)$$ (6.14)

The energy flow to the environment, as represented by equation 6.14, varies with time due to the changing internal and environmental conditions, and to the particular stage of the plant's development. However for a mature plant, the average energy output rate must equal the plant's average rate of accepting energy. Therefore, in general, the plant can be considered to be in energy equilibrium with the environment so that the flow of energy to the environment is balanced by an equal flow rate from the environment to the plant (i.e. accepted energy). Under these equilibrium conditions, the exchange energy can be determined from equation 6.14.

Short term variations and nonequilibrium conditions can be investigated by considering the differences between the emitted and accepted energy of a plant, and a transfer function associated with the plant. The relationship for the nonequilibrium condition are based on the general expressions for exchange energy developed in chapter III. Many of the considerations for mineral exchange energy under non equilibrium conditions, as developed in Chapter V, are valid for plants. For example, the transfer function shown in Figures 5-1 and 5-2 are equally applicable to plants and minerals.

To develop the transfer function for plants, let us again consider the basic relationship between the energy of a substance and the exchange energy as given in equation 3.21, i.e.:

$$e_s = e_{s0} + \int_0^t [\dot{e}_a(\tau) - \dot{e}_w(\tau)] \, d\tau$$ (3.21)

This equation states that the energy of a substance at some time t is equal to the energy of the substance at some reference time t_0 plus the change in the substance's energy between time t_0 and time t due to a net difference between the energy accepted by the substance and the energy emitted by the substance. The energy of the substance (e_{s0}) at the reference time is a constant, its value being dependent upon the state of growth and the stored energy of the plant. As the growth process is irreversible, the energy of the substance at some time t cannot be lower than the minimum internal energy that will sustain the plant at that particular stage of growth. This in effect establishes a limit on the term:

$$\int_0^t [\dot{e}_a(\tau) - \dot{e}_w(\tau)] d\tau.$$

For example, if a plant has obtained some particular stage of growth, then it requires a given amount of energy to maintain itself at that level. Falling below this minimum level results in death of the plant.

To adapt the general relationship given by equation 3.21 to plants, it is necessary to express the energy of the substance in terms applicable to plants. This can be achieved by using the expression for a plant's energy as given in equation 6.1. Combining equations 6.1 and 3.21 obtains:

$$e_{s0} + \int_0^t [\dot{e}_a(\tau) - \dot{e}_w(\tau)] d\tau = \sum_i \sum_j e_{sji} \qquad (6.15)$$

the desired form of the transfer function is a ratio of the energy flow rate out of the plant ($\dot{e}_w$) to the energy flow accepted by the plant ($\dot{e}_a$). To obtain this ratio, let us first differentiate equation 6.15 with respect to time as follows:

$$\dot{e}_a(\tau) - \dot{e}_w(\tau) = \frac{d}{dt}\left[\sum_i \sum_j e_{sji} \right] \qquad (6.16)$$

126

As e_{s0} is constant with respect to time, its derivative with respect to time is zero. Rearranging equation 6.16 obtains:

$$\dot{e}_w(\tau) = \dot{e}_a - \frac{d}{dt}\left[\sum_i \sum_j e_{sji}\right]$$

or

$$\dot{e}_w(\tau) = \dot{e}_a\left\{1 - \left(\frac{1}{\dot{e}_a}\right)\frac{d}{dt}\left[\sum_i \sum_j e_{sji}\right]\right\} \quad (6.17)$$

$$= \dot{e}_a H \quad (6.18$$

where H is the transfer function of the plant.

A more explicit form of equation 6.17 in terms of the phenomenon internal to a plant can be obtained by using equation 6.10 rather than 6.1 for the energy of the substance, i.e.:

$$e_s = \sum_i \sum_j e_{sji} = mc^2 + \sum_i \left(e_{seoi} + m_i \int_0^T C_i\, dT \right) + \sum_j M_j + \sum_k e_{fk} m_{0k} + Fm_{Fs} \quad (6.19)$$

Differentiation of equation 6.19 with respect to time will give the short term variations of the plant's energy as follows:

$$\dot{e}_s = \frac{d}{dt}\left[\sum_i \sum_j e_{sji}\right] = \dot{m}c^2 + \frac{d}{dt}\left\{\sum_i \left(e_{seoi} + m_i \int_0^T C_i\, dT \right) + \sum_j M_j + \sum_k e_{fk} m_{0k} + Fm_{Fs}\right\} \quad (6.20)$$

Equation 6.20 can be substituted into equation 6.17 to give a more explicit form of the short term transfer energy.

127

6.3.3 *Environmental Energy*

The local environment of a plant can be considered to be more restrictive than that for minerals because a plant cannot exist in as wide a range of energy conditions as a mineral. That is, the environment that can be tolerated by a plant is restricted, e.g., extreme temperatures will kill most plants. In addition, due to the reproduction criteria for a living organism, a plant's local environment will contain other plant individuals of the same species.

Due to the characteristic of plant species which allow them to adapt to slow changes in their local environment, in an evolutionary sense, they cannot, in general, exist in a local environment which changes drastically in one generation. Except for the requirement for a somewhat restrictive environment, the local environmental energy of a plant is the same as that considered in the general environment discussed in Chapter III and that considered for minerals in Chapter V.

6.3.4 *Functional Relationships*

A functional diagram for a plant-environment energy system can be constructed based on the plant energy equations and the substance-environment energy system block diagram given in Figure 3-8. The functional equation for a plant's energy is given by equation 6.10 and can be used directly in the block diagram. The energy released to the environment by the plant is given by equation 6.14. This equation can be used directly in the block diagram. The functional relationship for the environmental energy can be expressed in the same form for plants and minerals. Therefore the expression for environmental energy shown in Figure 5-4 can be used for plants.

A functional expression for the energy accepted by a plant is complicated due to the differences in the energy acceptance process between green plants, which can accept solar energy, and the nongreen plants. That is, the green plants can assimilate food from minerals and solar energy but the nongreen plants must depend on the existance of organic material for their food.

The acceptance of food energy from the environment can be expressed in functional form as $f(e_e, e_s, \theta)$, where θ represents the anabolism process of the plant. The plant also accepts heat energy, etc., much as a mineral does. The acceptance of this energy is dependent on the same atomic process as a mineral and can be expressed a $\Sum \frac{1}{2}h\nu_i$ where the summation is for all molecules of the plant.

A functional diagram for the energy of a plant-environment energy system, based on the foregoing energy considerations, is shown in Figure 6-1.

6.3.5 Directed Internal Energy

To obtain the internal knowledge of a plant, the portion of the internal energy which is directed by the plant must be determined. That is, the subset of the internal energy expressed in equation 6.10 which is operated upon, i.e., directed, by the plant must be determined. The individual energy terms in this equation are considered in the following dissertation to determine if that particular term represents directed energy.

I submit that the atomic energy due to the mass of the plant is not directed in any way. This energy, as represented by the term mc^2, is not changed or utilized by the plant in any manner.

The next term in the right hand side of equation 6.10 is a representation of the ground state potential energy of the molecules which constitute the plant. I argued in Chapter V that the ground state potential energy of a mineral molecule was not directed energy. As a plant is composed of molecules constituted from simpler elements and molecules, it should follow that the ground state energy of the molecules which makes up a plant is not directed by the plant. Independent of this argument, if a plant could exist when its molecules are in the ground state, this condition would represent the lowest possible energy level of the plant for a particular stage in its development, hence the potential energy below the ground state is not available to the plant and therefore cannot be directed by the plant. Therefore, I believe that the term

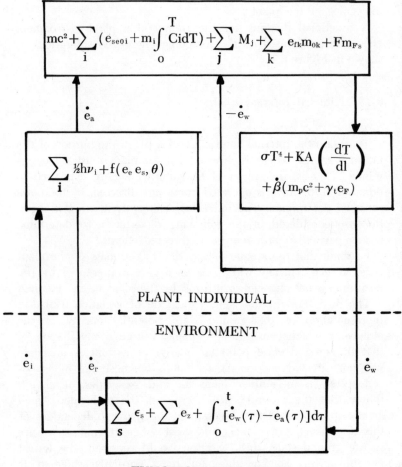

FUNCTIONAL DIAGRAM
PLANT SYSTEM ENERGY

Figure 6-1

130

$$\sum_i e_{se0i}$$

does not represent directed plant energy.

The internal heat energy of the plant is given in equation 6.10 by the term

$$\sum_i m_i \int_0^T C_i \, dT$$

where m_i and C_i are the mass and the specific heat of the ith molecule in the plant. If the mass (m) and the specific heat (C) of the plant can be determined at some point in time, then this equation becomes just:

$$m \int_0^T C \, dT \qquad (6.21)$$

It should be understood that the mass and probably the specific heat of a plant changes during its growth period and to a limited extent during its mature period. Some of the internal heat energy must be directed by the plant to maintain a thermal relationship with the environment. The amount of heat energy directed by a plant must depend on the temperature range in which the plant is considered to exist. For example, if a plant cannot exist below a given temperature, then the remaining heat between this point and absolute zero cannot be considered as being directed by the plant. By the same reasoning, if a plant cannot exist above a given temperature, then the heat energy between this temperature and the temperature at which the molecules of the plant dissociate cannot be considered as being directed by the plant. The temperature range over which a plant can exist may vary widely between plant species, e.g., some plants have been known to exist at temperatures in the neighborhood of absolute zero; existence being defined here as the capability to meet the metabolic and reproductive criteria in a normal temperature environment after having been subjected to the low temperatures (Ref. 6.9).

To show the heat energy for the range of temperatures where the plant can exist let us consider the heat energy expression in three parts as follows:

$$m \int_{0}^{T} C \ dT = m \int_{0}^{T_1} C \ dT + m \int_{T_1}^{T_h} C \ dT + m \int_{T_h}^{T} C \ dT, \qquad (6.22)$$

where T_1 and T_h are the lowest and the highest temperatures respectively that a specific plant individual can exist. I submit that the heat energy represented by;

$$m \int_{T_1}^{T_h} C \ dT \qquad (6.23)$$

can be directed by the plant. This amount of energy would be the maximum heat energy the plant could direct. To obtain the directed energy under normal conditions, the upper limit of this integral would be replaced by the expected or normal temperature.

The energy that can be obtained by the plant from foods that it stores internal to its structure is all directed energy. The foods can be stored in forms such as sugars, starches, and fats. A plant has the capability of extracting a certain amount of energy from a unit mass of the food which depends mainly on the type of food. The energy obtained from these foods by the catabolic process has been processed or changed by the plant and therefore is considered to be directed energy. As an example of the potential energy stored in foodstuff, consider the storage of sugar of the form given in equation 6.11. The one molecule of sugar, when combined with the proper amount of oxygen has the potential of releasing energy.

I submit that the mechanical energy represented by the term ΣM_j in equation 6.10 is a result of the metabolic process of the plant or the structural organization of the plant and therefore is directed energy. For example, the energy due to the movement of liquids through a plant due to osmosis, various differences in chemical composition, and capillary action are

132

all due to the functions and organization of the plant. That is to say, these energies would not be present if the plant did not exist; the amount of energy being a function of the particular organizational structure of a given plant species. The form and type of this energy is sensitive to the type of plant species and does not readily lend itself to generalized formulae. As an example of this dependence on the form of plants, it is obvious that the capillary action in large plants with veins differs greatly from this action in small one cell plants without veins.

I consider the organization, or formation, energy of the plant, as given by equation 6.7, to be directed energy. Indeed this represents a significant quantity of directed energy.

Based on the preceding arguments, the directed internal energy of a plant is given by the following equation:

$$e_{ds} = m \int_{T_1}^{T_h} C \, dT + \sum_j M_j + \sum_k e_{tk} m_{0k} + F m_{FS} \qquad (6.24)$$

6.3.6 *Directed Exchange Energy*

A plant directs some of the energy exchanged between itself and the environment. The central issue is the determination of the subset of exchange energy that is directed by the plant. As in the determination of the total exchange energy of a plant; described in Paragraph 6.3.2, it is desirable to consider both the steady state and the short term exchange energy.

It was shown in Paragraph 6.3.2 that the steady state transfer energy could be obtained by using the equation for the emission of energy into the environment; namely equation 6.14. To determine the amount of this energy which is directed by the plant, let us first consider the range of conditions under which the plant can exist. Using the arguments given in Paragraph 6.3.5, we see that the plant cannot exist at temperatures which are lower than T_1 or higher than T_h. Therefore for directed energy, equation 6.14 is valid only for the range of temperature between T_1 and T_h for the specific plant species under consideration. It can again be argued that the mass energy is not directed by the plant, therefore the mass energy, as represented by the term $m_p c^2$ in equation 6.14, is not directed energy. Deleting the mass energy and establishing the boundary conditions for equation 6.14, we obtain:

$$\dot{e}_w = \sigma T^4 + KA \ \frac{dT}{dl} + \beta \dot{\gamma} \ e_F \qquad T_1 \leqq T \leqq T_h \qquad (6.25)$$

I believe the steady state exchange energy derived from equation 6.25 to be the directed exchange energy for a plant. Due to the lower temperature limit, T_1, it is seen that a plant must have some exchange energy with the environment just to exist, providing of course that we exclude those rare cases of plants that may possibly survive at absolute zero degrees temperature.

Let us now consider the directed short term exchange energy. The total short term energies are given by equations 6.17 and 6.20 where the latter equation gives the short term variations in the internal energy of a plant. In the discussion on the internal directed energy, it was stated that the mass energy and the ground state electronic energy are not directed by the plant. In addition, it was stated that only a part of the heat energy was directed; the resulting directed internal energy is given by equation 6.24. Differentiation of equation 6.24 with respect to time will result in the short term changes in internal directed energy as follows:

$$\dot{e}_{sd} = \frac{d}{dt} \left\{ m \int_{T_1}^{T_h} C \ dT + \sum_j M_j + \sum_k e_{fk} m_{ok} + F m_{Fs} \right\} \qquad (6.26)$$

Equations 6.24 and 6.17 can be combined to obtain a relationship for directed short term exchange energy, i.e.;

$$\dot{e}_w = \dot{e}_a \left\{ 1 - \left(\frac{1}{\dot{e}_a} \right) \frac{d}{dt} \left[m \int_{T_1}^{T_h} C \ dT + \sum_j M_j + \sum_k e_{fk} m_{ok} + F m_{Fs} \right] \right\} \qquad (6.27)$$

134

This equation relates the accepted energy, the emitted energy and changes in the internal energy of the plant.

Let us investigate some of the important characteristics of the accepted energy and the methods whereby a plant can accept energy. The rate of accepting energy, $\dot{e}_a$, by a plant is a function of the energy available from the environment and the characteristics of the plant. It was shown in Paragraph 6.1 that the methods of accepting energy from the environment vary between plant species, e.g. the green plants can accept energy directly in the form of solar radiation while the nongreen plants obtain energy by oxidizing materials. All plants have the capability of accepting mass. That is, there is a flow of mass across the surface of the plant.

The short term energy exchange equation given in Chapter III (3.17) can be rewritten as follows;

$$\dot{e}_a = \dot{e}_s + \dot{e}_w .\tag{6.28}$$

The term $\dot{e}_w$ is the rate of expending energy and is directly associated with plant catabolism and radiant energy. The catabolism of a plant species is related to the size of the plant, temperature, nutrients, etc. Catabolism can be measured for a plant under a given set of conditions; the catabolism process being sufficiently well known that the rate of energy utilization can be predicted for a given set of conditions.

The accepted energy (e_a) for the green plants is related to the photosynthesis process. The summary equation for the photosynthesis process is:

$$6CO_2 + 6H_2O + energy \longrightarrow C_6H_{12}O_6 + 6O_2$$

The accepted mass is the 6 molecules of carbon dioxide (CO_2) and the 6 molecules of water (H_2O). The radiant energy is accepted by the plant. If we know the rate of photosynthesis, then we can calculate the accepted energy.

When a plant's metabolism stops, e.g., due to low temperature, its mass becomes constant leaving only thermal radiation effects which can be expressed as follows:

$$\dot{e}_a = \frac{d}{dt} \left[m \int_{T_1}^{T_h} C \, dT \right] \tag{6.29}$$

The accepted energy in a given time internal can be expressed as

$$e_a = \int_{t_1}^{t_2} \dot{e}_a \, dt \qquad\qquad (6.30)$$

This accepted energy can be in the form of solids (in solution), liquids, gases and radiant energy.

The rate of accepting energy can be determined from metabolic measurements, given the characteristics and the internal state of the plant. The rate of accepting energy is a function of the state of the plant, i.e., the organization and amount of stored internal energy. The rate of accepting energy is of major importance for three states of the plant. First, we are interested in the acceptance rate when the substance is in the lowest energy state for the particular state of plant organization. This is the rate that will just sustain life when there is no stored energy in the plant. Secondly, we are interested in the acceptance rate (metabolic rate) when the plant is in its normal mode. Third, we are interested in the greatest acceptance rate that the plant can experience.

6.3.7 *Directed Environmental Energy*

Plants can direct environmental energy only in a restricted sense. They can reject radiant energy and other energy directed at them by the environment, and through the process of growth a plant can displace mass in the environment. The rate of rejecting energy at any given instant of time was shown in Chapter V to be $\dot{e}_r$ for mineral substances. This expression is equally valid for plants as they exhibit similar radiant energy absorption phenomena as minerals. The methods that plants utilize in rejecting energy are more diverse than for minerals and are a function of a particular plant species. We are interested in the rejection of energy under normal conditions for a given plant species and in the maximum energy that can be rejected before the plant will expire.

136

A plant directs environmental energy when it displaces environmental mass in the growth process. The amount of energy directed by this process is a function of the pressure that can be generated in the plant by the growth process. At any instant of time, the amount of pressure and the amount of displacement due to growth can be determined. Therefore, the amount of directed environmental energy can be determined.

6.3.8 *Total Plant Knowledge*

The knowledge of a specific plant individual can be obtained from the directed internal, exchange, and environmental energy by adding these energies to obtain the total directed energy and then applying the basic knowledge directed energy equation to obtain the total knowledge of the plant.

The directed energy expressions for plants, as developed in the proceeding paragraphs, can be used to construct a functional diagram as shown in Figure 6-2. This diagram shows the functional relationships for that portion of a plant system's total energy which is directed by the plant.

°6.4 *Plant Information*

Plant information is indeed an interesting phenomenon. During each generation, sufficient information is passed from the parent plant to the offspring, through a single cell, to control the organizational energy of the offspring. That is, the organizational knowledge is passed from one generation to another through a single cell. Although this phenomenon is interesting, it is not central to the theory of knowledge and therefore is not treated in depth herein.

The subject of heredity, i.e., the transmission of hereditary characteristics, was discussed in qualitative terms by various nineteenth century philosophers. Hegel's "ESTHETIC" published in 1835 and Spencer's "PRINCIPLES OF BIOLOGY" published in 1864 are notable examples of the qualitative discussions of heredity during this era.

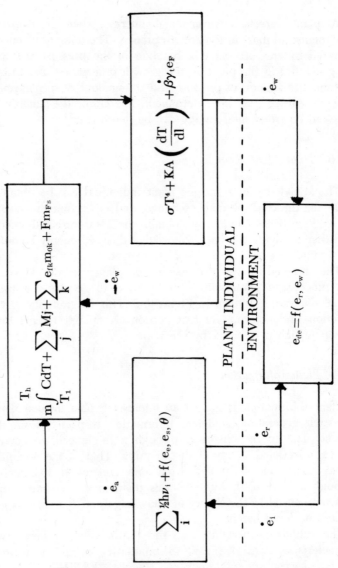

FUNCTIONAL DIAGRAM
PLANT SYSTEM DIRECTED ENERGY

Figure 6-2

138

Quantitative investigation of the transmission of hereditary information was initiated by Gregor Mendel in 1865. However, Mendel's laws were ignored until they were rediscovered, independently by Hugh de Vries, Correns, and Tschermak in 1900. These laws form the beginning of formal genetics. By this time, the chromosomes were identified as the celluar organelle responsible for the maintenance and transmission of the inheritable characters, and each gene was assigned a specific place on the chromosome. In 1944, Avery, MacLeod, and McCarthy identified the chemical desoxyribonucleic acid, or DNA, as the genetic material. In 1953, Watson and Crick discovered the structure of DNA.

Max Delbrück constructed a theoretical model of the mechanism for the transmission of hereditary characteristics based on theoretical physics. Delbrück's model was tested and extended by Erwin Schrödinger in his book "WHAT IS LIFE" (1944). Schrödinger concluded that an aperiodic molecule fulfills the requirements for a genetic material. That is, it has the capability of possessing the code-script necessary to pass on hereditary characteristics, has the stability required to maintain the code in the normal thermal environment, and fulfills the necessary condition that it can undergo mutation.

The investigations of the transmission of hereditary characteristics have resulted in the conclusion that each organism contains a structure, desoxyribonucleic acid (DNA), which is the basis of hereditary order. DNA contains the information for the production of specific templates and of specific proteins. This concept of the method of communicating hereditary information is compatible with the concept of knowledge presented in this book.

The reader who is interested in the details of hereditary information is referred to André Lwoff's book "BIOLOGICAL ORDER" (Reference 3.5).

*6.5 *Examples of Plant Knowledge*

The principles of plant knowledge are demonstrated by two examples in this paragraph. The first example shows the application of the principles to a single cell plant, bacteria. The second example applies the principles to trees. The reasons for selecting these particular plants are stated, the essential characteristics of the plants are described, the energy relations are determined, and the knowledge of the plants is calculated. Both the normal operating and the survival knowledge are calculated in the single cell example. Only the operating knowledge level is calculated in the tree example.

*6.5.1 *Bacteria Knowledge*

The major characteristics of bacteria and the relationship between bacteria and other plants can be described using the system of plant classification.

Bacteria are in the sub kingdom thallophyta (plants not forming embryos) and are in the phylum: Schizomycophyta (bacteria). The thallophyta sub kingdom have the following characteristics:

1. The sex cells are produced in rather simple sex organs
2. They do not form embryos
3. They do not have true roots, stems and leaves
4. There is a relatively slight degree of difference in tissue (no phloem, xylem, cambium, etc. in most kinds)
5. They are mainly water plants. (Land plants are mainly parasites or saprophytes)

Thallophyta is commonly considered as two great divisions. 1) Sub phylum A- algea and 2) Sub Phylum B - fungi. Algea have chlorophyll, fungi do not. Bacteria are in the fungi sub phylum. The fungi sub phylum have the following characteristics:

1. They lack chlorophyll
2. Most species are saprophytes or parasites or both
3. A few species make food by chemosyntheses (oxidation of certain chemicals supply the energy for food synthesis)
4. They do not have true roots, stems and leaves
5. They do not have vascular tissue
6. They do not form embryos.

140

The subphylem: fungi, is separated into three phyla:

1. Schizomycophyta (Bacteria)
2. Myxomycophyta (slime molds) and
3. Eumycophyta (true fungi).

Reason for Selection

Bacteria was selected for the following reasons:

1. They are the smallest living creatures known
2. All bacteria are unicelluar
3. They are the most widely distributed of all organisms; in water, air, soil, on and in other living organisms
4. They have three simple shapes; spheres, rods and spirals.

It will be convenient in some cases to use the general characteristics of bateria to illustrate the principles of knowledge. In other cases, where more specific characteristics are required, the genus, Streptococcus will be used. The streptococcus is classified as: Order I- Eubacteriales; Family VII; Lactabacteriaceae; Tribe I, Streptococcaceae; Genus II, Streptococcus, (Reference 6.7). The streptococcus was selected due to its small size, simple shape and it has been studied rather extensively.

Essential Characteristics

The essential characteristics of plants are listed in Paragraph 6.2.2. These characteristics for bacteria in general are as follows:

1. Mass. The mass of a micro-organism can be obtained at a given stage of growth by knowing the size and the constituents of the organism. The average size of bacteria is about 2 microns in length and ½ micron wide. Almost all of the mass is made up of oxygen, carbon, and hydrogen; in this order. (Reference 6.8).

2. Temperature. Bacteria does not seem to exhibit a lower survival temperature. J. Mac Fadyan and S. Rowland found that organisms survived temperatures as low as — 252°C (Reference 6.9). That is, the organisms were capable of development when the thermal environment was restored to the normal incubation temperature. There is a minimum temperature below

which an individual organism will grow. For the majority of bacteria, this temperature is between 5° and 6°C. Some marine and soil bacteria are active below 0°C, but this is exceptional. Bacteria exhibit optimum growth (energy absorption) at "normal" ambient environmental conditions. For soil organisms this temperature is about 25°C; for animal parasites, it is about 37°C. All bacteria cease to survive when the temperature exceeds a particular high value for a given organism. The energy (temperature-time) which causes death is some 10° to 15°C higher than the maximum growth temperature. The bacteriologists have arbitrarily chosen the death temperature as the lowest temperature which, when applied for exactly ten minutes, will destroy every individual in a fluid suspension of the organism. The death temperature for many organisms is between 38° and 48°C.

3. Basal Metabolism. The major metabolic requirements of bacteria are: favorable temperature, water, organic matter and the presence or absence of oxygen, depending on the species being either aerobic or anaerobic. Most bacteria require sugar or other material, such as the higher alcohols which can readily be converted into sugar, to build up their body substance. Most bacteria require nitrogen in combination with organic matter for their metabolic process. Some bacteria can assimilate energy at a rate that will allow reproduction as often as once every 20 minutes.

4. Surface Energy Transfer. Bacteria have no mouth parts or excretion parts, Therefore, their food must be imbibed in soluble form by diffusion through the cell walls and the metabolic byproducts must be excreted in soluble form by diffusion through the cell walls.

5. Extraction of Energy from the Environment. Some bacteria are motile; that is, they have a capability to move about under their own power. The motile bacteria can change their local environment by moving to another location.

Bacteria excrete enzymes which act on material in the environment to convert this material into forms that can be absorbed by the bacteria.

142

Streptococcus

The essential characteristics of streptococcus which differ from the general bacteria characteristics are:

1. Mass. The streptococci has a spherical shape with an average diameter of about 0.7 microns (Reference 6.7).

2. Metabolism. Streptococcus can be parasites and/or saprophytes. The streptococcus grow very well in dextrose brain broth, blood agar and litmus milk culture mediums. (Reference 6.7).

3. Motile. Streptococcus are non motile.

Internal Knowledge

To illustrate the application of the theory of knowledge to single cell bacteria organisms, let us consider four energy conditions corresponding to: the lowest energy that will allow the organism to survive, the energy at which metabolism starts, the maximum metabolism condition, and energy conditions which results in death of the organism. The internal energy of the organism for these four conditions can be obtained by evaluating equation 6.24 under the proper conditions.

Minimum Internal Knowledge

Let us determine the energy and knowledge of a bacteria cell in its lowest energy state. We see from the essential characteristics listed previously that some bacteria can exist as an organism at temperatures as low as $-252°C$. It is possible that bacteria may be able to survive at absolute zero degrees ($-273°C$). If this is the case, the minimum internal energy (e_s) is obtained by evaluating equation 6.24 at $-273°C$. From the essential characteristics of bacteria it is seen that the metabolic process stops at $0°C$, therefore the metabolic dependent terms of equation 6.24 can be neglected for the minimum internal knowledge case. Thus, equation 6.24 becomes:

$$e_d = m \int_{T_1}^{T_h} C\, dT + \sum_k e_{fk} m_{0k} + F m_{Fs}$$

143

At a temperature of absolute zero, the thermal energy becomes zero. Therefore the integral term in the above equation is zero.

The organizational energy term is evaluated by assuming the average energy per unit mass is 6 kilo calories per gram. This value of the energy per unit mass is based on a carbohydrate having 4 kilo calories per gram and a fat having 9 kilo calories per gram. Based on this assumption, and the mass of the streptococcus, the organizational energy can be calculated. The mass of the bacteria genus streptococcus is calculated as follows: from the essential characteristics, we have an average diameter of a streptococcus cell of 0.7 microns, resulting in an average cell volume of 1.8×10^{-13} cubic centimeters. Using the assumed specific gravity of 1 gram/cubic centemeter, the mass becomes 1.8×10^{-13} grams. The organization energy is calculated as follows: (6 kilo calories/gram) ($1.8 \times^{-13}$ grams) $= 1.08 \times 10^{-9}$ calories or 4.52×10^{-9} Joules.

The total directed internal energy under these assumptions is due to the organism's organization and is seen to be 4.52×10^{-9} Joules. The internal knowledge being utilized by the bacteria under these conditions is 4.52×10^{-9} knowledge units.

Minimum Internal Life Knowledge

A plant is considered to have life when it fulfills the metabolic criteria. The metabolic process for most bacteria starts between $5°$ and $6°C$ (see essential characteristics) while some start at $0°C$. For an assumed value of $0°C$ for the temperature at which growth just starts, the internal energy due to metabolism is essentially zero. Therefore, for minimum life conditions, equation 6.24 becomes:

$$e_d = m \int_{-273}^{0} C\,dT + \sum_{k} e_{fk} m_{0k} + F m_{F_s} \qquad (6.31)$$

It is assumed that the bacteria cell under consideration has recently undergone mitosis and that the lower energy state has been approached in such a manner that any stored energy, in the form of fats, oils, sugar, etc., has been used up by the

144

organism. These assumptions assure that the cell is in a minimum mass configuration. It is further assumed that the cell has the same specfic gravity and specific heat as water. These assumptions will simplify the calculation and still serve the purpose of illustrating principles. Under the specific heat assumption, the value of the integral in equation 6.31 can be determined from the area under the curve in Figure 6-3 for the temperature range -273 to $0°C$. Under these assumptions and for a cell mass of 1.8×10^{-13} grams, the directed internal energy of the streptococcus cell is:

$$e_d = (1.8 \times^{-13} \text{ g.}) \ (71 \text{ cal/g.}) \ (4.816 \text{ Joules/cal}) + 4.52 \times 10^{-9}$$
$$= 5.3 \times 10^{-11} + 4.52 \times 10^{-9} = 4.57 \times 10^{-9} \text{ Joules.}$$

The knowledge associated with this directed internal energy is:

$$k = (1 \text{ Joule}^{-1}) \ (4.57 \times 10^{-9}) = 4.57 \times 10^{-9} \text{ knowledge units.}$$

The minimum knowledge level for an "average" bacteria can be obtained in the same manner as illustrated above for streptococcus. It is assumed that the "average" bacteria is 2 microns in length and has a circular cross section of ½ micron diameter. The assumption on specific gravity and specific heat are the same as stated above for streptococcus. The volume of this average bacteria is 3.94×10^{-13} cubic centimeters and the mass is $3.94 \times^{-13}$ grams. Under the same assumptions as those used for streptococcus, we obtain the following value for the directed energy of an "average" bacteria cell:

$$e_d = (3.94 \times 10^{-13} \text{g}) \ (71 \text{ cal/g}) \ (4.186 \text{ Joules/cal}) +$$
$$(3.94 \times 10^{-13} \text{g}) \ (6 \times 10^3 \text{ cal/g}) \ (4.186 \text{ Joules/cal})$$
$$= 1.17 \times 10^{-10} + 9.896 \times 10^{-9} = 1.1 \times 10^{-8} \text{ Joules.}$$

The internal knowledge of the "average" bacteria due to this internal directed energy is: $K = 1.1 \times 10^{-8}$ knowledge units.

Normal Internal Knowledge

To obtain the normal internal energy, we must evaluate equation 6.24 at the expected average temperature of the bacteria. For bacteria such as streptococcus, this temperature is approximately $37°$ C. The maximum internal energy of the cell under

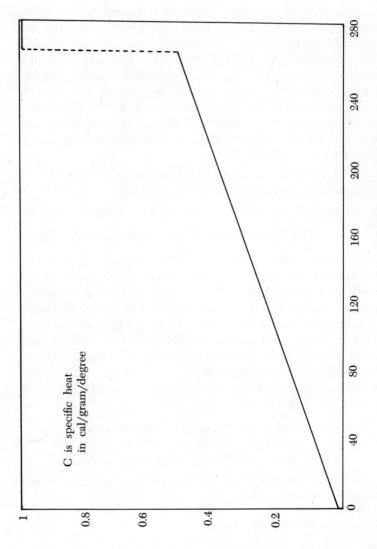

SPECIFIC HEAT OF WATER

Figure 6-3

146

normal conditions occurs just prior to division into two daughter cells and when the cell is growing at a maximum rate. The mass of the cell at mitosis is assumed to be double the "normal" mass of the streptococcus cell, i.e., the mass is equal to 3.6×10^{-13} grams.

Evaluation of the temperature component of equation 6.24 at the normal, i.e. the optimum growth temperature, obtains:

$$m \int_{-273}^{37} C \, dt = m \int_{-273}^{0} C \, dt + m \int_{0}^{37} C \, dT$$

$= 9.6 \times 10^{-11}$ Joules $+ 3.6 \times 10^{-13}$ (1 cal/deg/g) ($37°$) $\times$ (4.186 Joules/cal)
$= 9.6 \times 10^{-11} + 5.55 \times 10^{-11}$ Joules
$= 15.15 \times 10^{-11}$ Joules.

For simplicity, it is assumed that the streptococcus cell does not have stored food, therefore the stored energy term, Fm_{Fs}, will be zero. The organizational energy for the maximum condition will be twice that of the normal cell due to the mass being assumed to be doubled at mitosis. Therefore, the organizational energy is 9.04×10^{-9} Joules.

The term, ΣM_j, of equation 6.24 must be considered for bacteria in a normal environment. Metabolism is the sum total of the activities, growth, maintenance, and repair of the organism, and is a major cause of the energy represented by this term. These energies include radiant and thermal energies accepted by the cell, nutrients accepted into the cell, energies of chemical reactions resulting from metabolism, and the kinetic energy caused by diffusion of the metabolic products out of the cell. Metabolism influences the internal energy of the organism by (1) increasing the mass of the organism, (2) increasing the temperature due to the chemical reactions of metabolism, and (3) causing certain materials internal to the organism to have velocity, i.e., the diffusion of nutrients into and byproducts out of the cell.

The internal energy relations as a function of mass, concentration of substances, rates of reactions, etc. are given in Reference 6.10. For our purpose, we can show by a simple calculation that the internal energy due to the velocity of metabolic materials is negligible compared to the other internal energies of the cell. It has been determined that young plant growth, i.e., meristematic plant tissue has a metabolic rate which is approximately the same as that for animals. It has been shown by experiment that animals have a metabolic rate of approximately 1000 kilogram calories per square meter per day (Reference 6.12). If it is assumed that this energy is extracted from carbohydrate at a value of 4 kilogram calories per gram, then 1000 kilogram calories can be extracted from 250 grams of carbohydrate. The mass flow through a plant, in the form of carbohydrate, is in the order of 250 grams per square meter per day. The area of the streptococcus cell, assuming the effective area is the surface area of a sphere with a diameter of 0.7×10^{-4} cm, is:

$$A = \pi D^2 = \pi \, (0.7 \times 10^{-4})^2 = 1.54 \times 10^{-8} \text{ cm}^2.$$

The mass flow through the streptococcie is, under the stated assumptions, approximately:

$$(250 \text{ grams/m}^2/\text{day}) \, (1.54 \times 10^{-8} \text{cm}^2) \, (10^{-4} \text{m}^2/\text{cm}^2)$$
$$= 3.85 \times 10^{-10} \text{ grams/day} = 4.45 \times 10^{-15} \text{ grams/sec.}$$

Assuming that the mass flowing through the cell is not more than 10% of the "normal" mass of the cell at any one time, i.e., 1.8×10^{-13} grams, then 1.8×10^{-14} grams of the cell's mass is involved in the mass flow at any instant of time. If 1.8×10^{-14} grams are considered to be one mass unit, then there are approximately 0.25 mass units per second flowing through the cell. As the cell is 0.7×10^{-14} cm long, one mass unit will be assumed to be contained in this size. Therefore, the mass is flowing through the cell at rate of approximately (0.25 mass units/sec) $(0.7 \times 10^{-4}$ cm/mass unit)

$$= 1.75 \times 10^{-5} \text{ cm/sec.}$$

The kinetic energy due to metabolism is:

$$e = \tfrac{1}{2}mv^2 = \tfrac{1}{2}\,(1.8 \times 10^{-14}\text{ grams})\,(1.75 \times 10^{-5})^2$$
$$= 2.75 \times 10^{-24}\text{ ergs} = 2.75 \times 10^{-31}\text{ Joules.}$$

This value of energy is insignificant in comparison with the other internal energy of the cell.

The total internal energy under optimum growth conditions is:

$$e_d = 1.515 \times 10^{-10} + 9.04 \times 10^{-9} = 9.19 \times 10^{-9}\text{ Joules.}$$

The knowledge associated with this energy is:

$$k = 9.19 \times 10^{-9}\text{ knowledge units.}$$

Maximum Survival Internal Energy

As the environmental thermal energy increases, the growth rate of the bacteria starts to decrease and the bacteria dies when the temperature is $10°$ to $15°$ C above the optium growth temperature. As the cell can be in a maximum mass configuration, i.e., just prior to mitosis, and the metabolic energy can be neglected, the change in internal energy is determined by the temperature dependent term and the organizational energy term in equation 6.24. The directed energy becomes:

$$e_d = 9.6 \times 10^{-4} + 3.6 \times 10^{-13}\,(1\text{ cal/g/deg})\,(48) \times$$
$$(4.186 \times 10^7\text{ erg/cal}) + 4.52 \times 10^{-2}\text{ ergs.}$$
$$= 9.6 \times 10^{-4}\text{ ergs} + 7.2 \times 10^{-4}\text{ ergs} + 4.52 \times 10^{-2}\text{ ergs}$$
$$= 4.69 \times 10^{-9}\text{ Joules.}$$

The knowledge associated with the energy is 4.69×10^{-9} knowledge units.

Exchange Knowledge

To illustrate the application of the plant exchange energy and knowledge equation, let us consider the energy states and conditions that were used in determining the internal knowledge; namely, the lowest energy that will allow the organism to survive; the lowest energy at which metabolism starts; the maximum metabolism condition; and energy conditions which result in death of the organism. The directed energy for these conditions can be obtained by evaluating the emitted directed energy equation, 6.25, under the proper set of constraints.

Minimum Exchange Knowledge

It is again assumed that the bacteria can exist at zero degrees Kelvin (absolute zero). This assumption is based on experimental verification that certain bacteria can exist at temperatures as low as $-252°$ C ($21°$ Kelvin) and the likelihood that certain bacteria can exist at $0°$ K. Using the fact that metabolism in bacteria stops at $0°$ C, the metabolic rate will certainly be zero at $-273°$ C. Evaluation of equation 6.25 under these conditions results in no directed exchange energy being required by the bacteria. As the directed exchange energy is equal to zero, the exchange knowledge will be equal to zero.

Minimum Exchange Life Knowledge

The directed exchange energy of bacteria in an energy state just below the start of metabolism can be obtained by evaluating equation 6.25 for a temperature of zero degrees centigrade. As metabolism has not started, then the term due to metabolism in equation 6.25 must be zero. The remaining directed energy terms are due to radiant and conducted energies.

To obtain crude estimates of directed exchange energy under the conditions of a zero degree environment, it is assumed that the radiation properties of the streptococcus cell are the same as those of a black body radiator and that the cell is surrounded by air with a thermal coefficient of 5.68×10^{-5} (Reference 4.1). The radiation and conduction area of the streptococcus is assumed to the same as that calculated for the normal internal knowledge, i.e., 1.54×10^{-8} cm². An additional assumption is made which will result in large values for the conduction energy, namely that the temperature falls to absolute zero in a distance of one centimeter. This will cause a temperature gradient larger than would be experienced in nature. Under these assumptions, the emitted energy as given by equation 6.25 becomes:

$$\dot{e}_w = (5.672 \times 10^{-5} \text{ ergs/cm}^2/\text{deg}^4/\text{sec}) \ (1.54 \times 10^{-8} \text{ cm}^2) \times (273 \text{ deg})^4 + (5.68 \times 10^{-5} \text{ cal/sec}^2/\text{cm/deg}) \ (1.54 \times 10^{-8} \text{ cm}^2) \times (4.186 \times 10^7 \text{ ergs/cal}) \ (273 \text{ deg/cm})$$

$$=4.84\times10^{-3}+10^{-2} \text{ ergs/sec}$$
$$=1.5\times10^{-2} \text{ ergs/sec or } 1.5\times10^{-9} \text{ Joules/sec.}$$

To obtain the directed energy emitted into the environment in a given time interval, the energy rate must be integrated with respect to time. As in the case of a mineral's directed exchange energy, the second is selected for the standard time interval. For a one second time interval, the emitted energy is 1.5×10^{-9} Joules. This energy results in an exchange knowledge of 1.5×10^{-9} knowledge units.

Normal Exchange Knowledge

To obtain the exchange knowledge level for normal conditions of a bacteria individual and its environment, equation 6.25 is evaluated for expected or normal conditions of temperature and metabolic processes. The radiant and conduction energy emitted to the environment is obtained by evaluating the first two terms in equation 6.25 for the normal temperature. If we assume the that individual streptococcii is an animal parasite, then its normal temperature is $37°$ Centigrade or $310°$ Kelvin.

The form of the metabolic term in equation 6.25 does not readily lend itself to calculation due to a lack of good data. Instead, extrapolation will be made based on certain experimental data. A crude estimate of the energy released by catabolism will be based on experimentaly determined relations between the rate of catabolism and the superficial area of an organism. The catabolism process is essentially the same for all living things (Reference 6.4) and the amount of energy catabolized is a function of the superficial area of the living organism. Indeed, it has been determined that young plant growth, i.e., meristematic plant tissue, has a metabolic rate that is approximately the same as that for animals (Reference 6.11). It has been shown by experiment that animals have a metabolism rate of approximately 1000 kilogram calories per square meter per day (Reference 6.12). Assuming that

151

this rate applies to streptococcii, the energy rate can be calculated as follows;

catabolism rate $= (1000$ kg cal/m^2/day) (area in m^2) (day/sec)
$$= (10^6) \ (1.54 \times 10^{-8}) \ (10^{-4}) \ (1/8.64 \times 10^4)$$
$$= 1.78 \times 10^{-11} \text{ calories/second or}$$
$$7.46 \times 10^{-11} \text{ Joules/second.}$$

The total emitted energy is obtained as follows;

$$\dot{e}_w = (5.672 \times 10^{-5}) \ (1.54 \times 10^{-8}) \ (310)^4 + (5.68 \times 10^{-5}) \times$$
$$(1.54 \times 10^{-8}) \ (310) \ (4.186 \times 10^7) + 7.46 \times 10^{-18}$$
$$= 8.06 \times 10^{-3} + 1.13 \times 10^{-2} + 7.46 \times 10^{-18} \text{ ergs/sec}$$
$$= 1.94 \times 10^{-9} \text{ Joules/sec.}$$

The amount of exchange energy for normal conditions and for a one second time interval is; $e_w = 1.94 \times 10^{-9}$ Joules which results in a value of exchange knowledge equal to 1.94×10^{-9} knowledge units.

Maximum Survival Exchange Knowledge

As the internal temperature increases in the streptococcii from its normal condition, the metabolic processes slows until it essentially stops prior to the death of the streptococcii. We are interested in the value of the directed exchange energy just prior to the death of the streptococcii, i.e. the maximum survival directed exchange energy. As we have stipulated that the metabolic process has stopped, the emitted energy is due only to radiation and conduction. This energy can be obtained by evaluation 6.25 at a temperature of 321° Kelvin and for no metabolic rate as follows;

$$\dot{e}_w = (5.672 \times 10^{-5}) \ (1.54 \times 10^{-8}) \ (321)^4 + (5.68 \times 10^{-5}) \times$$
$$(1.54 \times 10^{-8}) \ (321) \ (4.186 \times 10^7)$$
$$= 9.3 \times 10^{-3} + 1.17 \times 10^{-2} \text{ ergs/sec}$$
$$= 2.1 \times 10^{-9} \text{ Joules/second.}$$

This directed energy yields exchange knowledge of 2.1×10^{-9} knowledge units.

Environmental Knowledge

Bacteria can direct environmental energy by the process of growth and by rejecting radiant environmental energy. In the growth process, the cell can displace a volume equal to the growth in the cell provided the internal forces generated by the cell are greater than the pressure exerted on the cell by the environment. The internal pressures generated by a cell will differ depending on the size of the cell, cell structure, etc. In our example, we chose the mature cell therefore the displacement due to growth is essentially zero.

The streptococcii chosen for a example is an animal parasite and therefore is not exposed to solar radiation. As the streptococcii is not subjected to solar radiation, it does not direct this type energy. Therefore, in our example, the streptococcii does not direct enviromental energy.

Knowledge of the Streptococcii

The knowledge level of the streptococcii for the various stated conditions can be obtained by summing the internal, the exchange, and the environmental knowledge for these stated conditions.

Minimum survival knowledge: There is a high probability that certain bacteria can exist, i.e., survive, at temperatures approaching absolute zero. It was shown that for a temperature of absolute zero, the bacteria has only organizational knowledge, i.e., 4.52×10^{-9} knowledge units. That is, the bacteria is operating at zero exchange and environmental knowledge conditions at absolute zero degrees temperature. This knowledge level is much lower than the bacterium's total knowledge capability.

Minimum life knowledge: The minimum life knowledge, i.e., the knowledge level the stroptococcii is using under the energy conditions where metabolism just starts, is the sum of the internal and the exchange knowledge; enviromental knowledge for our example being zero. This knowledge level is;

$$k=4.52\times10^{-9}+1.5\times10^{-9}=6.02\times10^{-9} \text{ knowledge units.}$$

It should be noted that the conducted exchange directed energy accounts for a significant part of the knowledge. However, the conditions for determining the conducted energy are not very representative of conditions expected in nature, therefore the knowledge calculation should be considered for illustration purposes only.

Normal (expected) knowledge: The normal or expected knowledge level is that most likely to be found in nature. Due to the adaptive nature of plants, the expected value of knowledge is likely to be near the maximum knowledge capability of the plant. That is, the plant adjusts to its environment so that it can direct the most exchange energy under these normal conditions of environment. As the directed exchange energy seems to be the predominant factor, it appears that the maximum directed energy, hence knowledge, occurs under conditions of a normal environment. The value of the normal knowledge level for the streptococcii example is;

$$k=9.19\times10^{-9}+1.94\times10^{-9}=11.1\times10^{-9} \text{ knowledge units.}$$

Maximum survival knowledge: This knowledge level represents that which is used by the streptococcii just prior to expiring due to high thermal energy conditions. This knowledge is:

$$k=4.69\times10^{-9}+2.1\times10^{-9}=6.79\times10^{-9} \text{ knowledge units.}$$

6.5.2   Tree Knowledge (Giant Sequoia)

To further illustrate the application of knowledge theory to plants, an example is given for the largest known plant, namely the Giant Sequoia. The Giant Sequoia's knowledge level is calculated for the expected conditions of the tree and its environment. In addition, certain, simplifying assumptions are made to make the calculations more tractable.

The major characteristics of trees and their relationship to other plants can be described in terms of plant classification. The Giant Sequoia tree is in the sub kingdom - Embryophyta (plants forming embryos), the phylum tracheophyta (plants with vascular tissues), the sub phylum - pteropsida (ferns and seed plants), the class Gymnospermae (cone bearing plants), the order - Coniferales, the family - Taxoodiaceae, the sub family - Tasodioideae, the genus - Sequoiademdron, and the specie - Sequoiadendron geganteum (Giant Sequoia).

Reason for Selection

The tree represents the opposite end or the plant spectrum from bacteria as they are the largest living creatures known and they synthesize their own food. The Giant Sequoia was selected as it is the world's most massive living organism and may possibly be its oldest. The tree also represents the most developed plant organism, having true root, stem and leaf systems.

Essential Characteristics

The essential characteristics of the Giant Sequoia follow:
1. Mass. The mass of the Giant Sequoia is indeed very large. The largest Giant Sequoia specimen is the General Sherman in Sequoia National Park. The mass of this tree is estimated to be 2150 tons, of which the foliage alone constitutes 155 tons (Reference 6.13).
2. Temperature. The survival temperature range of a mature Giant Sequoia is not easily determined due to the inability to perform controlled experiments on such a massive organism. The temperature range of the current natural environment can be determined; however, these trees attain ages in excess of 3000 years and the average temperature of the natural environment may have changed in this time period. The Giant Sequoia is native only to the westerly slope of the Sierra Nevada in California, principally at altitudes between 5000 to 8000 feet.
3. Metabolism. Green plant metabolism is divided into anabolism (building up of substance) and catabolism (destruction of substance). The basic anabolism process (photosynthesis) can be shown by the summary equation:

$$6CO_2 + 6H_2O + \text{radiant energy} \longrightarrow C_6H_{12}O_6 + 6O_2 \ .$$

The summary catabolism (respiration) equation is:

$$C_6H_{12}O_6 + 6O_2 \longrightarrow 6CO_2 + 6H_2O + \text{energy}.$$

For a plant to survive, the long term rate of photosynthesis must be equal to or greater than the long term rate of respiration. That is, the average amount of sugar synthesized during a photosynthesis period must be equal to or greater than the sugar reduced by respiration during a 24 hour period. Normally, the material synthesized is much greater than the material reduced.

Internal Knowledge

The internal knowledge level at which the Giant Sequoia normally operates can be determined by evaluating the internal directed energy equation under expected or normal conditions, and then calculating the internal knowledge based on this directed energy. To evaluate equation 6.24 (internal directed energy), it is necessary to obtain the mass, the temperature, the specific heat, the stored food energy, the efficiency of converting stored food energy to usable energy, and the miscellaneous energies of the tree.

For illustration purposes, let us use the General Sherman tree because data is more readily available for this particular tree than most Giant Sequoias. From the essential characteristics, it is seen that the mass of the General Sherman is 2150 tons or 1.95×10^9 grams. The specific heat of wood is given in Reference 4.1 as 0.42 calories per gram per degree. The lower temperature, T_1, that a Giant Sequoia can withstand and still live is not readily available data. I would doubt that the sequoia can withstand extremely low temperatures; however, in the absence of data and to have a comparison among examples, a lower temperature of absolute zero will be used. The normal operating temperature of the tree is assumed to be $290°K$ which is the ambient temperature of the earth. The heat term of equation 6.24 can now be evaluated as follows:

$$m \int C \ dT = mCT \Big|_{T=0}^{T=290°K}$$
$$= (1.95 \times 10^9 \text{ g}) \ (0.42 \text{ cal/g/deg}) \ (290°\text{K})$$

which is equal to 2.38×10^{11} calories or

9.95×10^{11} Joules.

The stored food in the General Sherman tree can vary from season to season and at any time is probably not known with any degree of certainty. It is conceivable that the stored food could vary from zero up to probably 15% of the tree's total mass. For purposes of illustration, one percent of the tree's total mass will be assumed to be stored food in the form of sugar, i.e., 1.95×10^7 grams of sugar. The usable energy of a carbohydrate is usually taken to be 4 large calories, i.e., 4 kilogram calories, per gram (Reference 6.14). Therefore, the stored potential energy in our example is;

$$e = Fm_{Fs} = (4 \text{ kg cal/g}) \ (1.95 \times 10^7 \text{ g}) = 7.8 \times 10^{10} \text{ calories}$$
$$= 3.26 \times 10^{11} \text{ Joules.}$$

Had the stored food been fat, the energy would be more than double the amount of energy shown for carbohydrate as the energy in fat is approximately 9 large calories per gram.

The miscellaneous energy term in equation 6.24, i.e., ΣM_j, includes the increased heat in the tree due to metabolism, the energy of fluid movement in the tree due to osmosis, capillary, etc. One of the major causes of fluid flow in a tree is the transpiration process whereby water is absorbed from the soil by osmosis and transported up through the roots and trunk to the leaves where it is expelled into the atmosphere. The internal kinetic energy due to this fluid flow can be obtained by determining the mass and velocity of the fluid flowing in the tree. The transpiration rate of temperature zone plants can range up to 5 grams per square decimeter of leaf area per hour (Reference 6.15). The leaves of the Giant Sequoia are scale-like, sharp pointed, and never exceed one half (½) inch in length. The leaves average between one eighth and one fourth inch in length. The leaves overlap, the lower leaf tending to shield the lower part of the upper leaf (Reference 6.16). The base of the leaf is approximately one half its length. To determine the weight of the average leaf, it is assumed to be triangular shaped with a length of three eighth inches, a base of three sixteenths inch, a thickness of 0.016 inches, and that it has an average density of 0.036 pounds per cubic inch. Therefore, the area of one side of the leaf is 0.035 square inches, the volume of the leaf is 5.6×10^{-4} cubic inches, and the weight of the average leaf is 2.02×10^{-5} pounds. Assuming the total mass of the foliage to be 155 tons as reported by Fry and White (Reference 6.13), we obtain the number of leaves on the General Sherman as:

$$N = \left[\frac{(155 \text{ tons}) \ (2000 \text{ lbs/ton})}{2.02 \times 10^{-5} \text{ lbs}} \right] = 1.54 \times 10^{10} \text{ leaves.}$$

Assuming the total area of the leaf is twice the single side area, the total foliage area of the General Sherman is (2) $(0.035)(1.54 \times 10^{10}) = 10.78 \times 10^{8}$ square inches, which is equal to 6.95×10^{9} square centimeters, or 6.95×10^{7} square decimeter.

If it is assumed that the average transpiration rate is 2 grams per square decimeter of leaf area per hour, then the total rate of transpiration of the General Sherman is $(2 \text{ g/dm}^2)(6.95 \times 10^{7})$ $= 1.39 \times 10^{8}$ grams per hour. According to the U.S. Government Printing Office pamphlet "The Giant Sequoias of California" by Lawrence F. Cook, the General Sherman is 272.4 feet to the top of the trunk and it is 129.9 feet to the first large limb. It is assumed that the average height of the leaves is approximately 200 feet above the ground. Even if it is assumed that the transpired mass moves the total distance of 200 feet in one hour, the velocity is only 1.69 centimeters per second and the energy is:

$e = \frac{1}{2}mV^2 = \frac{1}{2}(1.39 \times 10^{8}\text{g})(1.69\text{cm/sec})^2 = 1.98 \times 10^{8}\text{ergs}$
$= 19.8$ Joules.

It is seen that this energy is negligible compared to the thermal and the stored potential energy.

The basic organizational energy of the General Sherman is

obtained by evaluating the organizational energy term in equation 6.24. As the basic organizational energy has been identified with the minimum mass for a particular stage of plant growth, the mass associated with stored food energy, i.e., fat, is not considered in the computation of the organizational energy. The stored food energy has been considered earlier. Assuming that the organizational energy per unit mass of the tree averages 6 kilogram calories per gram and that the mass is equal to the total mass less the stored food mass, i.e., an organizational mass of 1.92×10^9 grams, then the organizational energy is:

$$(6 \times 10^3 \text{cal/g})(1.92 \times 10^9 \text{g})(4.186 \text{ Joules/cal})$$
$$= 4.82 \times 10^{13} \text{ Joules.}$$

The total internal energy of the General Sherman, under these assumptions is the sum of the energies calculated above, i.e.,

$$e_d = 9.95 \times 10^{11} + 3.26 \times 10^{11} + 4.82 \times 10^{13} \text{ Joules}$$
$$e_d = 4.9 \times 10^{13} \text{ Joules.}$$

The knowledge associated with this directed energy is
$k = 4.90 \times 10^{13}$ knowledge units.

Exchange Knowledge

The normal exchange knowledge of the General Sherman is obtained by evaluating equation 6.25 for normal conditions to obtain the directed exchange energy and then calculating the knowledge associated with this directed energy. The temperature dependent terms in equation 6.25 can be determined in much the same way as that used for bacteria; however, it will be more convenient and instructive to obtain the metabolic exchange energy by determining the accepted metabolic energy.

To obtain a crude approximation of the thermal energy that must be supplied by the environment, the thermal portion of equation 6.25 is evaluated assuming that the tree is releasing energy into an absolute zero degree environment. As the radiant and the conduction energy are a function of the superficial area of the tree, we will procede to approximate this area. The approximate area of the foliage was determined in the paragraph on internal knowledge to be 6.95×10^9 square centimeters. To determine the superficial area of the trunk, it is assumed that the trunk is conical and smooth. By Reference 6.17, the General Sherman's trunk is 272.4 feet high, 30.7 feet in diameter at its base, and 17 feet in diameter at the 120 foot height. The surface area of a cone is:

$$A = \pi R \sqrt{R^2 + h^2}$$

where R is the radius at the base and h is the height of the cone. Therefore, the area of the General Sherman's trunk, under these assumptions is:

$$A = \pi 15 \sqrt{(15)^2 + (272)^2} = 1.28 \times 10^4 \text{ square feet,}$$

or 1.19×10^6 square centimeters. The area of the trunk is negligible compared to the area of the foliage.

The radiant energy is calculated using the total radiating area of the tree and assuming that the tree is a perfect radiator as follows:

$$\sigma T^4 = (5.672 + 10^{-5} \text{ergs/cm}^2/\text{deg}^4/\text{sec})(6.95 \times 10^9 \text{cm}^2)(290)^4$$
$$= (3.94 \times 10^5)(7.08 \times 10^9) = 2.79 \times 10^{15} \text{ ergs/sec}$$
$$= 2.79 \times 10^8 \text{ Joules/second.}$$

To obtain a crude approximation of the energy emitted by conduction, several assumptions must be made. It is assumed that the tree is surrounded by air with a thermal conductivity of 5.68×10^{-5}. The rate of releasing energy by conduction will be estimated for the condition where the temperature of the tree is at $290°$K and the environmental temperature is absolute zero at a distance of one foot from the tree. Under these assumptions, the rate that heat energy is being conducted to the environment is:

$$KA \left(\frac{dT}{dl} \right) = (5.68 \times 10^{-5})(6.95 \times 10^9) \left[\frac{290°\text{K}}{12 \times 2.54} \right]$$

$$= 3.76 \times 10^6 \text{ calories/second or } 1.57 \times 10^7 \text{ Joules/sec.}$$

It should be noted this energy rate represents a rather special set of conditions and is not very representative. If the energy emitted from the tree were not replaced, a typical cooling curve would result. As a practical matter, the energy emitted from the tree is immediately replaced by energy accepted from the environment.

Accepted Energy

The acceptance energy of green plants was discussed in Paragraph 6.3.5 in relationship to photosynthesis. Photosynthesis can be defined as a function of the various environmental factors such as temperature, intensity of radiant energy, available nutrients, etc. The actual calculations of the photosynthesis process for a large plant under normal environmental conditions is difficult if not impossible. This is due to the normal variations in temperature, variations in the amount of received solar energy caused by cloud cover and shadowing from other foliage, uncertainty in the amount and form of nutrients, etc. However, as our purpose is only to illustrate principles, simplifying assumptions are made to obtain gross numerical estimate of the accepted energy.

The rate of photosynthesis is generally controlled by the pace of the slowest factor. F. F. Blackman's (1905) "Principle of Limiting Factors" makes the following statement, "When a process is conditioned as to its rapidity by a number of separate factors, the rate of the process is limited by the pace of the 'slowest' factor" (Reference 6.18). In general, carbon dioxide is the limiting factor in photosynthesis; constituting only 0.03% by volume of the atmosphere.

Assuming that carbon dioxide (CO_2) is the limiting factor, the products of photosynthesis can be calculated for the General Sherman. The rate of photosynthesis as a function of light intensity is given by Figure 6-4 (Reference 6.5).

To simplify calculations, let us assume that the photosynthesis rate is 3 mgs of CO_2 per 100 cm^2 of leaf surface per hour and that the photosynthesis period is 8 hours in each 24 hour period. The total leaf area exposed to direct sun light at any one time is very difficult to obtain. However, if the leaf area exposed to sunlight and the intensity of the sunlight were known, then

161

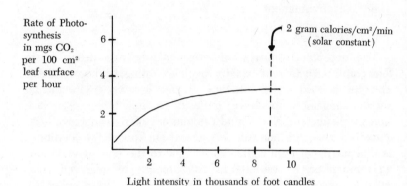

PHOTOSYNTHESIS RATE vs. LIGHT INTENSITY

Figure 6-4

the maximum carbon dioxide synthesized in the photosynthesis period could be obtained.

The amount of water required in the photosynthesis of CO_2 could be obtained from the summary equation:

$$6CO_2 + 6H_2O + \text{energy} \longrightarrow C_6H_{12}O_6 + 6O_2 \quad (\text{Reference } 6.18)$$

and the molecular weights of water and carbon dioxide. The ratio of the molecular weight of H_2O to CO_2 is approximately 0.4. Therefore, for each pound of CO_2 synthesized, (0.4) pounds of water are used. Based on these considerations, the material synthesized by the General Sherman could be estimated.

The radiant energy accepted by the tree could be calculated from the summary photosynthesis equation as the amount of material synthesized can be obtained and the energy required to synthesize 6 molecules of CO_2 is known.

Due to the many uncertainties in this method of obtaining the accepted radiant energy, it is desirable to use a simplified approach which will give a gross indication of the magnitude of the accepted radiant energy. The radiant solar energy near the earth is 2 gram calories per square centimeter per minute or 0.033 calories per square centimeter per second. Let us assume that this energy is incident upon an area which represents the maximum leaf area that can be presented by the General Sherman to the incident radiant solar energy. Certainly an area of 9×10^4 square feet is more than adequate to represent the effective radiant energy intercept area of the General Sherman as the projection of the tree on a plane is no greater than 300 feet by 300 feet. This area is equal to 8.36×10^7 square centimeters, which when multiplied by the incident energy, results in 2.76×10^6 calories per second falling on the effective area. Only a small percentage of this total incident light energy is utilized in the photosynthesis process. The percentage of incident light energy utilized varies between approximately 1.5 to 5 percent but rarely, if ever, exceeds 5 percent (Reference 6.19). Assuming a value of 2 percent, the maximum solar energy accepted by the General Sherman by the photosynthesis process is (2.76×10^6) (0.02) or 5.52×10^4 calories per second during the photosynthesis period. As the photosynthesis period usually does not exceed more than 8 hours in a 24 hour period, the average accepted energy per day by the photosynthesis process cannot exceed 1.84×10^4 calories per second averaged over a 24 hour period or 7.7×10^4 Joules per second in a 24 hour average.

Let us now assume that the system is in equilibrium; therefore, the energy used in catabolism is equal to the energy accepted due to anabolism when averaged over a 24 hour period. The rate of catabolism is therefore 7.7×10^4 Joules per second. As catabolism is a continuous process, it should be considered or a per second basis.

The knowledge level associated with this energy is:

$$k = \int_t^{t=1} 7.7 \times 10^4 \, dt = 7.7 \times 10^4 \text{ knowledge units.}$$

The total directed exchange energy for the General Sherman

is the sum of the individual terms of equation 6.25, i.e.,

$$\dot{e}_w = \sigma T^4 + KA \left(\frac{dT}{dl} \right) + \dot{\beta} e_F$$

$$= 2.79 \times 10^5 + 1.57 \times 10^7 + 7.7 \times 10^4 \text{ Joules/second}$$
$$= 2.9 \times 10^8 \text{ Joules/second.}$$

The total exchange knowledge level resulting from this directed energy is 2.9×10^8 knowledge units.

Environmental Knowledge

The Giant Sequoia can direct environmental energy by rejecting radiant energy and by displacing material during the growth process. The displacement of material due to growth is a very slow process and the resulting energy is negligible compared to the rejected radiant energy. Again, only a small percentage of the total light energy incident on a plant is utilized in the photosynthesis process. The percentage of incident light energy utilized varies between approximately 1.5 to 5 percent but rarely, if ever, exceeds 5 percent (Reference 6.19). Assuming a value of 2 percent for the utilized energy, the rejected energy becomes 98 percent. If the incident radiant energy is 11.55×10^6 Joules per second when averaged over a 24 hour period, then the rejected energy would be 11.32×10^6 Joules per second when considered on the same basis. The radiant energy is actually rejected during the photo period; however, it is convenient to consider it averaged for a 24 hour period and then converted to Joules per second. Under these assumed conditions, the environmental knowledge becomes 11.3×10^6 knowledge units.

Knowledge of the General Sherman

The operating knowledge level of the General Sherman, under the assumed conditions, is the sum of the internal, the exchange, and the environmental knowledge. It is seen that under the assumed conditions, the organizational knowledge is the predominant term, namely 4.9×10^{13} knowledge units. It is again cautioned that the numerical values are for illustration purposes only and should not be construed to be a determination of the actual normal knowledge level of the General Sherman.

Chapter VII

ANIMAL KNOWLEDGE

7.0 *Introduction*

A measure of animal knowledge is developed in this chapter. It is not my intent to develop all the equations and relationships for a complete determination of animal knowledge but to develop certain directed energy — knowledge relationships which will show, in general, how the theory of knowledge applies to animals. The basis characteristics of animals are reviewed, the directed energy of animals discussed, certain equations are developed for the animal's capability for directing internal, exchange, and environmental energy, and an example is given to show how certain directed energy — knowledge relationships apply to an animal. Man was selected as the animal for the example in order to show the application of knowledge theory to a highly developed animal.

7.1 *Characteristics of Animals*

As indicated in Chapter VI, an exact definition delimiting all animals from all plants is impossible. However, in general, an animal is a living organism that cannot synthesize carbohydrates and proteins from inorganic or simple organic substances, but must ingest them in complex forms as food. In addition, most animals are distinguished from most plants by freedom of spatial movement.

In many respects, animals have the same characteristics as plants. They both are living organisms, and have the capability of assimilation and respiration, reproduction, growth and development, movement, and secretion and excretion.

167

7.1.1 *Morphological Characteristics*

The detail morphological characteristics of animals are of importance to the theory of knowledge as they assist in differentiating one species from another. It is also important to know gross morphological characteristics in order to assess the degree of an animal's organization.

Single Cell Animals

One major group of animals are those composed of a single cell. As a cell represents the smallest living organism, these unicellular animals represent the lowest degree of animal organization.

The unicell animals have many sizes and shapes. Some are simple spheres, other have elongated bodies and rudimentary mouth parts, etc.

Multi-cellular Animals

The second large group of animals are those composed of many cells. The multi-cellular animals range from those with a small amount of organization to those considered as higher animals having highly developed tissue and organs.

7.1.2 *Physiological Characteristics*

Animals cannot synthesize their food but must depend on the pre-existence of organic substance. As these organic substances are the product of other living substances, the animal is essentially a parasite on existing plant and animal life. Another general characteristic of animals is growth and size limitations. A given member of an animal species obtains a particular size at maturity and then maintains approximately this size for the remainder of its life.

We are interested in the physiological characteristics which relate to the transfer of energy between an animal and its environment, the energy transformations internal to the animal, and those energy transformations in the environment which are caused by the animal.

Physical

All animals must obtain physical substances from the environment. This substance is both organic and inorganic; the organic material is the animal's food, the inorganic; materials include oxygen, water and certain minerals. In addition, all animals must have a thermal energy exchange with the environment. The cold blooded animals (heterothermic) must obtain thermal energy from the environment for survival. The warm blooded (homoiothermic) animals are not quite so dependent on the environment thermal energy. Indeed, one could conceive of a warm blooded species adapting to a relatively low thermal environment.

The methods of obtaining physical substance from the environment vary over a wide range depending on the animal species. However, the final usage of the physical substances are in the individual cells where the processes are essentially the same for all animals.

Chemical

The chemical processes involved in changing materials from the environment into other forms and into energy is normally referred to as metabolism. Temperature, moisture, atmosphere, nutrients, and many other environmental factors affect the metabolism process. The primary metabolic process is essentially the same in all animals. That is, organic foods are reduced by combining with oxygen (burning). Indeed, the fundamental process of respiration is the same for all living things; plant or animal. The fundamental process for the metabolism of carbohydrates is given by the summary chemical equation:

$$C_6H_{12}0_6 + 60_2 \rightarrow 6C0_2 + 6H_20 + \text{energy} \tag{7.1}$$

In words, this equation states: one molecule of glucose plus six molecules of oxygen yield six molecules of carbon dioxide plus six molecules of water plus energy. The actual chemical process is more complicated than shown in the summary equation, there being intermediate metabolism stages and enzyme actions.

169

Carbohydrates, fats, and proteins are the major energy producing foods. The metabolism of fats and proteins are not as simple as that for carbohydrates due to the more complicated molecular structures of the fats and proteins, and more complicated chemical reactions involved.

Metabolism is influenced by such factors as species, race, age, sex, climate, season, and size, to mention a few (Reference 7.1).

7.2 Classification of Animals

The system of classifying animals is the same as that used for plants. The present classification system for living things was established by Carolus Linnaeus (1707–1778). This system provides an insight into the structure and characteristics of animals. A detailed discussion of the classification system is beyond the scope of this book. The reader is referred to any general book on biology (e.g., Reference 7.2).

For our purpose, we are interested in those characteristics that differentiate one species from another, that define the energy relations with the environment and that determine the internal energy of the animal. More specifically, we are interested in the essential classification and characteristics that allow the determination of animal knowledge to be made. These include: 1) mass, 2) temperature, 3) metabolism, 4) method of energy transfer between the environment and the animal, 5) method of extracting energy from the environment, 6) work done on the environment, 7) structural organization, and 8) method of transferring knowledge to another animal.

7.3 Energy-knowledge Relations for Animals

Many of the energy relations for animals are similar to those for minerals and plants. The important differences are the ability of animals to 1) move about rather freely in the environment, 2) perform work on the environment, 3) regulate their body temperature, and 4) sense the status of the environment and take rapid action. It should be recognized that some plants have a few of these listed properties. However, in general, these important differences exist between animals and plants. A few examples will illustrate exceptions to these differences between plants and animals.

Some single cell plants have the mechanisms for moving in their environment. However, in general, plants are not motile but animals are. Plants have a limited capability to perform work on the environment as seen by the movement of plant roots in the soil. Many animals (the cold blooded species) do not control their body temperature; however, plants do not have the capability of controlling body temperature. Some plants have the capability of sensing the environment and taking rapid action. Examples of plant sensing and action are sleep movements (closing of tulip petals, folding of leaves of clover, etc.) and the rapid movements of Venus' fly trap and sundew.

7.3.1 *Internal Knowledge*

The internal knowledge relationships of animals are not significantly different from those of plants. Indeed, it would be difficult to differentiate between the form of the internal knowledge equation for a one cell plant and a one cell animal. The higher plants and animals do exhibit differences in internal energies. The energy due to animal movement and the constant temperature characteristics of certain animals are examples of these differences.

The basic equation for the internal energy of plants, as developed in Chapter VI, is applicable to animals. The general logic and the basic equation (6.24) for the directed internal energy as developed for plants in the last chapter are directly applicable to animals. Due to the difference between higher plants and animals. the form of the summation terms of equation 6.24 is not quite the same for plants and animals. These differences are due to such factors as movements in animals and their change in internal energy as a result of performing work on the environment. The exact form of the summation term depends upon the type of animal, hence these forms of directed energy are not amenable to general treatment. These

171

forms of directed energy are shown for a specific animal in the example in this chapter.

7.3.2 *Directed Exchange Energy*

The general exchange energy relationships are similar for all living organisms. Therefore, the general exchange energy relationship developed for plants in equation 6.14 is applicable to animals when certain modifications are made. To apply this equation to animals requires a further specification of the individual terms of the equation to account for mechanical work performed by animals, the constant internal temperature conditions for warm blooded animals, etc.

The exchange energy for the steady state condition, i.e., for a mature individual under stable conditions, can be obtained by determining the directed energy flowing into the environment. Under steady state conditions, the energy released to the environment is equal to the energy accepted by the individual; the energy converted by the individual during this process is directed energy.

The energy passing from an animal to the environment, $\int \dot{e}_w \, dt$, consists of mass, heat, and mechanical energy. The mass transfer is a result of the by-products of metabolism passing to the environment, liquids utilized in cooling warm blooded animals, etc. The radiant energy is that passing to the environment in the form of thermal energy. Heat energy is also transferred to the environment by conduction and in the heat of the mass that is passed to the environment. The mechanical energy can be in the form of work performed on the environment and work performed in voluntary or involuntary mechanical movement of the animal.

The work performed by an animal on its environment can be included in equation 6.14 by considering the origin of the work energy. The energy released in the catabolism process of animals can be used for the growth process, the internal maintenance of the animal, the generation of heat, and the performance of mechanical work. The generation of heat which flows to the environment and the mechanical work performed on the environment are involved in the exchange energy between the animal and the environment. If that portion of the energy released to the environment by catabolism which is used in the generation of heat and in performing work on the environment is denoted as γ_h and γ_w respectively, then equation 6.14 can be rewritten as:

$$\dot{e}_w = \sigma T^4 + KA\frac{dT}{dl} + \dot{\beta}(m_p c^2 + \gamma_h e_F + \gamma_w e_F). \tag{7.2}$$

It is more convenient to rearrange equation 7.2 to combine the heat, mass, and work terms as follows;

$$\dot{e}_w = (\sigma T^4 + KA\frac{dT}{dl} + \dot{\beta}\gamma_h e_F) + \dot{\beta}m_p c^2 + \dot{\beta}\gamma_w e_F \tag{7.3}$$

where:

$$\sigma T^4 + KA\frac{dT}{dl} + \dot{\beta}\gamma_h e_F = \dot{e}_{wh} = \text{the rate of heat energy flowing into the environment,}$$

$$\dot{\beta}m_p c^2 = \dot{e}_{wm} = \text{the flow of mass energy into the environment,}$$

$$\dot{\beta}\gamma_w e_F = \dot{e}_{ww} = \text{the rate of expending mechanical energy on the environment.}$$

It is convenient to consider the heat energy flowing into the environment in two parts, namely $(\sigma T^4 + KA\frac{dT}{dl})$ and $\dot{\beta}\gamma_h e_F$. If the temperature in the first part, i.e. the term in brackets, is evaluated at ambient or standard conditions, then this term can be considered to be caused by non-metabolic heats. The second term, i.e. $\beta\gamma_h e_F$ can then be considered as due to the metabolic process and is the heat flow from the animal into an ambient or standard environment. Considered in this way, the latter term is equivalent to measured metabolic caloric flow. We can now write:

$$\dot{e}_w = \dot{e}_{wm} + \dot{e}_{wh} + \dot{e}_{ww} \tag{7.4}$$

or

$$\dot{e}_w = \int \dot{e}_{wm} dt = \int \dot{e}_{wm} dt + \int \dot{e}_{wh} dt + \int \dot{e}_{ww} dt \tag{7.5}$$

The term, $\dot{e}_{wm}$, on the right hand side of equation 7.4 (mass flow) is relatively predictable for a given species and is mainly a function of the metabolic rate of the animal. The term varies as a function of the age, growth rate, type of food, food habits, etc.; but within limits, can be predicted for a given species. There are also variations in mass flow due to the amount of mechanical work performed, climatic conditions, etc. For a mature member of a species, the mass flow rate under various conditions can be predicted rather well.

The mass transferred to the environment can be in the form of solids, liquids, and gas. For instance, animals pass solids as feces, liquids as urine and perspiration, and carbon dioxide as gas. The form and characteristics of the mass transferred to the environment is only partly dependent on the food eaten. Indeed, the human feces resulting from an exclusive rice diet may have nearly the same composition as that resulting from an exclusive meat diet (Reference 7.1). This is due to the feces being secreted from the alimentary tract (metabolism by-product) and the foods being almost completely digested. Large variations in the mass transferred to the environment can exist in cold blooded animals. These variations are due to the large variations in metabolic rate as a function of the thermal environment. As the mass energy, e_{wm}, i.e. atomic energy, is not controlled by the animal, it cannot be considered as directed energy.

The second term, $\dot{e}_{wh}$, on the right hand side of equation 7.4 (heat flow) is a function of the thermal characteristics of the animal (warm blooded, cold blooded, hybernating), species, environmental conditions, and changes in the environmental conditions. Heat can be transferred to the environment by radiation, conduction, heat of the mass flow to the environment, and heat added to the material that is accepted from the environment. The heat transferred by radiation and conduction is a function of the temperature of the animal, the temperature of the environment, the surface type and area of the animal, and the type of animal (cold blooded, warm blooded), to mention a few of the more important factors. The heat transferred by mass

174

is a function of the temperature of and the amount of mass leaving the animal.

There is a difference in the heat transferred to the environment between warm and cold blooded animals. The temperature of cold blooded animals varies with the thermal environment. At environmental temperatures between 1 to $20°C$, these animals are usually about $1°C$ warmer than the environment (Burns-Ref. 7.12). When the temperature of the environment exceeds a "normal" ambient temperature, the temperature of the cold blooded animals are usually somewhat lower than the environmental temperature. Due to the small thermal gradient between a cold blooded animal and its environment, there is not a large heat flow from the animal to the environment under normal conditions. The warm blooded animals maintain a constant temperature and therefore can have a temperature substantially different from that of the environment. Therefore, substantial amounts of heat can flow from these animals to the environment.

The last term $\dot{e}_{ww}$, on the right hand side of equation 7.4 (mechanical energy) is related to the ability of the animal to perform mechanical work on the environment. Mechanical work internal to the animal due to one part of the animal acting on another part cannot be regarded as work on the environment. This internal work appears as heat in the animal which may subsequently be transferred to the environment as heat energy.

The mechanical work performed on the environment includes walking, running, moving objects in the environment, working against gravity, obtaining food, etc. The ability of an animal to perform work on the environment is a function of the species, the structural form of the animal (arms, legs, hands, wings, paws, etc.), and metabolic capability.

The directed exchange energy can be obtained from the sum of the individual directed energies:

$$e_w = \int \dot{e}_w dt = \int \dot{e}_{wh} dt + \int \dot{e}_{ww} dt \qquad (7.6)$$

This equation can also be expressed as;

$$e_w = \int (\sigma T^4 + KA \frac{dT}{dl} + \dot{\beta}\gamma_h e_F) dt + \int \dot{\beta}\gamma_w e_F \ dt \qquad (7.7)$$

Certain animals, e.g., one cell animals, do not have the capability of performing work on the environment. For these animals, the last terms on the right hand side of equation 7.6 and 7.7 become zero. Under steady state conditions, equation 7.7 can be used to obtain the directed exchange energy for an animal.

Survival Energy

A certain amount of energy must be processed by the animal just to maintain basic organism functions. This minimum energy for maintenance is called basal metabolism. A generally accepted definition of basal metabolism for humans is the metabolic rate of an individual lying perfectly still, sufficiently long after a meal, so that no digestion is taking place, and at a temperature range between $30°$ to $35°C$. For our purposes, we can consider basal metabolism to be the energy flow rate required for an animal to exist under a given set of conditions for the animal and the environment. In general, basal metabolism energy flow rates are different from the energy flow rates which will just allow the animal to survive. We are interested in metabolism for conditions that will just allow survival. To illustrate the differences in basal metabolism for different internal conditions, let us consider the experiment Benedict (Ref. 7.3) performed with a squad of athletic men. These men whose normal daily intake was 3200–3600 calories, were placed on a diet containing 1400 calories for a period of three weeks. The men lost, on an average, 12 percent of their weight and their basal metabolism was reduced 18 per cent. The men were able to maintain this lower weight on 1950 calories per day, however, on this reduced intake, they were not as active as previously and had a lower tolerance of cold temperature.

Basal metabolism is a good measure for many applications but does not provide sufficient information to determine minimum energy flow throught an animal which will just allow the animal to survive. Basal metabolism provides a measure of only the term $\int \dot{e}_{wh} \, dt$ in equation 7.5 as basal metabolism measurements are made under rest conditions, i.e., $\int \dot{e}_{ww} \, dt = 0$. In addition, the measurement of basal metabolism is made under

176

ambient temperature conditions and therefore does not give the heat energy flow due to the thermal temperature of the environment. Also, basal metabolism is the metabolic rate of the animal in its current condition, whatever that condition may be, e.g., excess weight. We can write:

$$\text{Basal metabolism} = \int \dot{e}_{whb} dt \qquad (7.8)$$

where the subscript, b, indicates basal metabolism heat only.

The directed energy required for survival cannot be divorced from the energy conditions of the environment. However, we can standardize the environmental energy, as in the case of basal metabolism, to obtain comparative measures between animals. Let us assume a benign thermal environment, as is done in the case of basal metabolism, an abundant food supply so that mechanical energy is not required to obtain survival energy, and that the animal's internal energy is in the lowest possible state, i.e., no reserve fats or other energy. A standard survival energy can be obtained from equation 7.5 when evaluated under the above assumptions. This standard directed survival exchange energy for a given species can take the following form:

$$\int_{t}^{t+\tau} \dot{e}_w dt \quad , \quad \text{or} \quad \int_{t}^{t+\tau} \dot{e}_{wh} dt \qquad (7.9)$$

where τ is a standard time period, the mass of the animal is the minimum for survival, i.e., no fat, the temperature is standardized at 30° to 35°C, no work is being performed, i.e. $\int \dot{e}_{ww} dt = 0$, and all other environmental factors are "nominal" for the given species, i.e., the oxygen, moisture, etc., are typical to the environment the species normally inhabits.

The effect of environmental changes on the survival of a species is of interest. We want to be able to determine if a given animal species has sufficient exchange knowledge to survive under a particular set of environmental conditions or changes to these environmental conditions. The directed survival energy can be obtained from equation 7.7, evaluated under a given set of internal animal conditions and a given set of environmental conditions. For an energy condition which just allows survival,

177

we know that the mass of the animal is minimum. That is, all the reserve internal energy of the animal has been used up. The internal thermal energy must be completely specified for the given species in order to properly evaluate the directed exchange energy. The internal temperature at which an animal expires is a function of the species, e.g., a cold blooded animal can survive at internal temperatures of a few degrees centigrade whereas warm blooded animals expire when their internal temperature decreases from their normal temperature by a few degrees.

Once the internal conditions have been specified, the energy flow from the species can be determined. That is, we can determine the energy flow rates required to support the internal conditions of the animal. The heat flow rate must of course depend on the thermal environment. For example the heat flow will be much greater into a cold environment than into a warm environment. This phenomenon can be seen from the work of Horst, Mendel, and Benedict (ref. 7.4) on the metabolism of albino rats during prolonged fasting at environmental temperatures of $16°$ and $26°C$. Both groups of rats had an average weight of 222 grams at the beginning of the fast. The total metabolism of the individual rats kept at $16°$ was definitely higher (about 80 percent) than that of the animals kept at $26°C$. The metabolic rate of the group in the $16°C$ environment was rather constant while that of the group in the $26°C$ environment had an average decline of 36 percent on the seventh day. As a result, the loss in weight was more rapid in the group in the $16°C$ environment. The animals fasting in the $26°C$ environment survived on an average 16.5 days and lost 49 percent of their initial body weight, while the animals in the $16°C$ environment lost almost as much weight (44 percent) within a period of 11 days, this being the average survival time of this group.

The mechanical work, $\int \dot{e}_{ww} dt$, performed on the environment to obtain survival energy varies with the severity of the environment. If the environment is benign, very little work must be performed by the animal to obtain sufficient energy for survival. As the environment becomes more severe, the animal must expend more energy on the environment to obtain survival energy until a point is reached where the animal is expending mechanical energy at his maximum capability and he is still not able to obtain sufficient energy for survival.

It would appear that the larger and the more complex an animal, the greater the directed energy and knowledge required for survival. As an example, warm blooded animals which have complex heat regulating systems must direct more energy than cold blooded animals, and the larger an animal, the more heat it loses to the environment which the animal must replace by the metabolic process.

Nominal Directed Energy

A certain amount of directed exchange energy is required for a normal animal in its natural environment. Let us call the directed exchange energy under these conditions the nominal directed energy. To calculate the nominal directed exchange energy, the internal energy relations of the normal animal and the energy conditions of the natural environment must be completely specified. Due to the evolution process of animal species, the nominal directed energy is probably close to optimum for a given animal. The directed exchange energy can be obtained by evaluating equation 7.7 under normal conditions. To determine the tolerance of an animal to environmental changes, the ability of the animal to direct energy should be obtained as the environmental energy is increased and decreased about the nominal point.

Maximum Directed Exchange Energy Capability

An individual of an animal species has the capability of directing only a certain amount of exchange energy. In general the maximum capability will depend on such factors as size, surface area, mass, thermal conditions of the animal and the environment, morphological characteristics, etc. A typical mature animal of a given species will have certain internal energy conditions (i.e., mass, thermal, etc.). There will be variations about this set of internal energy conditions between the individuals of a

179

given species or race; however, these variations are not, in general, very large. For instance, in a warm blooded animal the body temperature and mass are almost constant, and the height and weight variation between individuals of a race do not normally vary greater than about 15 percent.

The maximum directed energy can be limited by the energy accepted from the environment, the energy released to the environment, or the internal energy of the animal. The total energy released by the animal cannot exceed the accepted energy for very long. The accepted energy in turn is limited by the capability of the animal to digest and reduce ingested nutrients. On the other hand, the maximum capability of the animal to direct mechanical energy is limited by the skeletal and muscular configuration of the animal. The amount of heat transferred to the environment is directly related to the surface area of the animal and to the environmental conditions. As an example, a larger amount of energy is required to maintain the body temperature (of warm blooded animals) in extremely cold climates than in a warm climate. Heat energy and mechanical energy are correlated because heat is generated in the expenditure of mechanical energy. The maximum directed energy capability can be calculated by using an exact specification of the characteristics of the animal and the environment. The value of maximum directed exchange energy can be obtained by evaluating equation 7.7 for extreme conditions.

Directed Exchange Energy vs Environment Energy

The preceding discussion of directed exchange energy was related to specific environmental conditions. An animal's directed energy, as a function of environmental changes is an important consideration in determining the knowledge level at which an animal operates.

In the preceding discussion, it was pointed out that directed energy is low when the environmental energy is low and that the optimum directed energy probably occurs in the "natural" environment of the animal.

The components of the environment that have first order

180

effects on the animal are: 1) temperature, 2) nutrients, 3) water, and 4) air. There are many environmental components which have lower order effects on an animal; they include the availability of certain minerals, solar radiation, and cosmic radiation. Based on the preceding discussion of minimum, nominal and maximum directed energy one would expect that the directed energy as a function of environmental energy would be of the form somewhat like that shown in Figure 7-1. The directed energy curve shown in Figure 7-1 is the result of all the independent environmental conditions that affect the animal. Curves of directed energy as a function of the thermal environment for warm blooded and cold blooded animals should take the form shown in Figures 7-2 and 7-3 respectively.

The shape of the curve in Figure 7-2 is caused by two phenomena. Below the nominal range, the animal must have a high metabolic rate to generate heat to replace the heat lost to the environment. The heat flow $\dot{e}_{wh}$ increases as the temperature is decreased below the nominal range. When the point is reached where the animal cannot maintain its body temperature due to the large amount of heat energy loss to the environment, it expires. Above the nominal range, the animal tries to maintain body temperature by transferring mass (mainly water) to the environment which in turn carries off heat energy. When the heat loss by the mass transfer cannot maintain the body temperature at its proper value, the animal expires.

The cold blooded animals maintain a body temperature approximately equal to that of the environment. Therefore, the curve in Figure 7-3 is approximately linear with temperature. When the environmental temperature reaches extremes which are greater than the animal can tolerate, the animal expires.

The general shape of the directed energy curve as a function of the nutrients in the environment should be of the form shown in Figure 7-4 for warm blooded animals or for cold blooded animals in a constant temperature environment.

The total directed energy shown in Figure 7-4 is a function of the availability of nutrients in the environment. The shape of the directed energy curve is governed by the availability of nutrients which can be absorbed and metabolized by the ani-

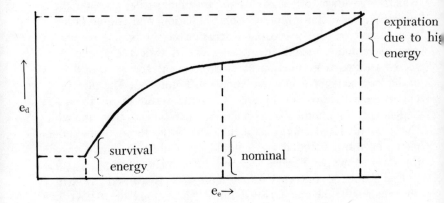

DIRECTED ENERGY vs ENVIRONMENTAL ENERGY
Figure 7-1

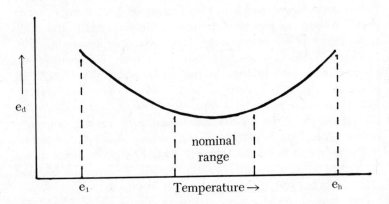

DIRECTED ENERGY vs TEMPERATURE FOR
WARM BLOODED ANIMALS

Figure 7-2

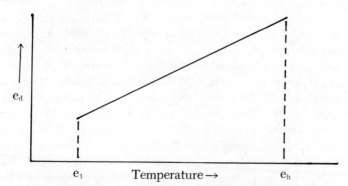

DIRECTED ENERGY vs TEMPERATURE FOR
COLD BLOODED ANIMALS

Figure 7-3

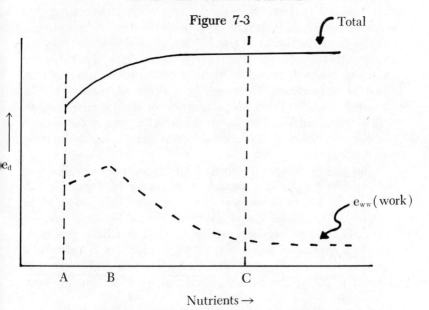

DIRECTED ENERGY vs NUTRIENTS

Figure 7-4

183

mal. The nutrients are sufficiently abundant above point C on the curve to provide the energy requirements of the animal. Normally, the animal will use only that which he requires. Below point C, the nutrients are less than required by the animal and hence his directed energy is restricted. As the nutrients decrease, the energy decreases till the point A is reached where the animal cannot sustain life, i.e., it starves to death.

The shape of the mechanical work curve shown in Figure 7-4 is a function of the energy expended by the animal to obtain nutrients. When the nutrients are in abundance (above point C), the animal does not perform much work in obtaining nutrients from the environment. As the nutrients decrease below point C, the animal must perform more and more work until a point is reached (B) where the animal is performing work at his maximum capability. Between points B and A, the animal is working at his maximum capability until he cannot sustain life (point A). However, his work capability is decreasing due to starvation, i.e., limited energy produced by catabolism.

The curves shown in Figure 7-4 are applicable under constant temperature conditions. The curves are directly applicable for a warm blooded animal as these animals maintain a constant internal temperature. There will be a family of curves for cold blooded animals which are a function of the internal temperature of the animal. This family of curves is due to the change in the metabolic rate of cold blooded animals as a function of temperature.

The general shape of directed energy curves as a function of environmental water should be as shown in Figure 7-5. If the water supply is abundant, i.e., greater than point C in Figure 7-5, the animal can easily obtain the required amount of water to satisfy his internal energy and metabolic processes. A given amount of water is required to carry on the metabolic processes at a given rate. The directed mechanical energy required to obtain the normal amount of water is normally relatively low.

As the amount of water available to the animal decreases from point C down to point B, the directed energy decreases due to decreasing metabolism. The mechanical energy directed in an effort to obtain water is increased as the water supply decreases. The increase in directed mechanical energy is due to the additional work required to obtain sufficient water to maintain body functions.

As the amount of water available to the animal decreases from point B to point A, the directed energy continues to decrease and the directed mechanical energy begins decreasing. The mechanical energy decreases due to the inability of the body to function properly during water starvation. At point A, there is not sufficient water to maintain body functions so the animal expires.

The general shape of the directed energy curves as a function of available oxygen in the environment is the same as for water and is shown in Figure 7-5. The values of the coordinates of the curve will be different for oxygen and water. It is a well known fact that an animal can go for hours and sometimes days without water but can go without oxygen for only a very few minutes.

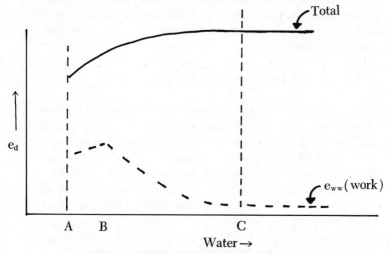

DIRECTED ENERGY vs WATER

Figure 7-5

There are other environmental energies which affect animals. These include solar, cosmic, and X-ray radiation, and various minerals. For the natural environment, these energies are of secondary importance. However, if the radiant energy becomes excessive, the organization of the animal becomes disrupted. Under these pathological conditions, the animal loses its ability to properly direct energy and subsequently dies. Changes in minerals absorbed from the environment can also result in pathological conditions in the animal, which if excessive, can cause death.

7.3.3 *Exchange Knowledge*

The exchange knowledge equations developed in previous chapters are applicable to animals. That is, exchange knowledge is equal to the directed exchange energy multiplied by a constant S; in the system of units selected for use in this book, the constant is equal to one.

It was shown in Paragraph 7.3.2 that directed exchange energy decreases as the available environmental energy decreases. Therefore, it follows that the knowledge level at which a given animal is operating decreases as the environmental energy decreases.

7.3.4 *Directed Environmental Energy*

All animals are capable of rejecting environmental energy at their surface in much the same manner as minerals and plants. The environmental energy rejected by the animal is considered to be directed environmental energy as the animal has operated upon this energy and changed its direction. In addition to rejected environmental energies, certain animals are capable of storing some of the environmental energy for use at a later time or for use by another animal, and of converting certain environmental energy for its own immediate use. These energies are considered to be directed environmental energy.

All animals must obtain food from the environment. Although some animals can obtain their required amount of food without

186

directing environmental energy, i.e., they obtain food from environmental energy impinging on the animal, most animals must direct environmental energy to obtain their required amount of food.

The form of the rejected energy is much the same as that for minerals and plants. A large portion of the energy rejected by most animals is in the form of radiant energy. The rate of energy rejection is denoted by $\dot{e}_r$. The capability for rejecting energy is a characteristic of the animal species.

Certain energy obtained from the environment is dependent on the work performed by the animal upon the environment. Also, the environmental energy impinging on the animal can be modified by the animal through the work process.

When an animal works on the environment to obtain energy which is used by the animal, then the environment can be represented by a function (λ). Some of the energy output from the animal is used to perform work on the environment which in turn results in energy which is used by the animal, therefore an energy system consisting of the animal and the environment can be represented by a feedback diagram as shown in Figure 7-6.

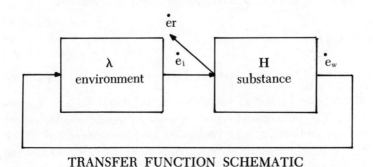

TRANSFER FUNCTION SCHEMATIC

Figure 7-6

The terms $\dot{e}_i$, $\dot{e}_w$, λ and G in Figure 7-6 are defined as:

$\dot{e}_i$ = the local environmental energy flow rate which acts on/or interacts with the substance.

$\dot{e}_w$ = the rate of flow of energy from the substance to the environment.

H = the transfer function of the substance.

λ = the transfer function of the environment.

Based on observation, it is apparent that $\dot{e}_i$ contains energy directed toward the substance which does not require effort on the part of the substance, e.g., radiant solar energy. In addition, $\dot{e}_i$ is a function of work performed on the environment by the substance, e.g., food which requires work to obtain, ingest, and digest. The local environmental energy which acts on the substance can be expressed in equation form as:

$$\int \dot{e}_i dt = \int \dot{e}_\alpha dt + \int \dot{e}_\beta dt \qquad (7.10)$$

$\dot{e}_\alpha$ = the rate at which environmental enery is directed toward the substances with no expenditure of energy by the substance.

$\dot{e}_\beta$ = the rate at which environmental energy is directed toward the substance as a result of an action by the substance.

Equation 7.10 can be rewritten in terms of rates as:

$$\dot{e}_i = \dot{e}_\alpha + \dot{e}_\beta$$

The rate at which environmental energy is directed toward the substance as a result of action by the substance ($\dot{e}_\beta$) is a function of the amount and type of energy in the local environment and the amount of work performed on the environment. If we let $f(e_e)$ be a functional representation of the amount and the type of energy in the environment which can be worked on by the animal, then we can write:

188

$$\dot{e}_\beta = f(e_e)\dot{e}_w \qquad (7.11)$$

Based on equation 7.11, the input flow rate can be expressed as:

$$\dot{e}_i = \dot{e}_\alpha + f(e_e)\dot{e}_w$$

or

$$\dot{e}_i = \left[\frac{\dot{e}_\alpha}{\dot{e}_w} + f(e_e) \right] \dot{e}_w \qquad (7.12)$$

The term in the bracket in equation 7.12 is in the form of a transfer function for the environment and can be represented as λ. Therefore it is possible to write:

$$\dot{e}_i = \lambda \dot{e}_w \qquad (7.13)$$

where

$$\lambda = \left[\frac{\dot{e}_\alpha}{\dot{e}_w} + f(e_e) \right]$$

Let us relate the terms in equation 7.12 to actual physical phenomena. The energies directed toward the substance which require no effort from the substance, $\dot{e}_\alpha$, include: 1) solar radiation, 2) cosmic radiation, 3) heat, 4) gravity, and 5) ambient gas and liquid pressures. Many of the environmental energies are reasonably constant when considered on a large scale. For instance, the solar radiation near the earth can be considered constant, the heat content of the earth is relatively constant, and mass energy of the earth is relatively constant. In addition, these environmental energies are so large compared to those of a given animal or substance that they can be considered as infinite energy sources and energy sinks with respect to the animal.

Many of the local environmental energies are far from constant as can be seen by the daily solar energy variations caused by the rotation of the earth. In addition, an animal can change the amount of energy it receives by moving to another location where the local environmental energies are different. The animal is not required to expend energy to receive this type energy from the environment but it must expend energy to change the amount of energy it receives. The local environment can be considered in two categories; 1) those that can not be modified by action on the part of the animal, e.g., gravity effects, and 2) those that can be modified by an expenditure of energy by the animal, e.g., shielding from solar radiation falling on the animal. Energies in the first category are completely contained in the $\dot{e}_{\alpha}$ term of equation 7.12. Energies in the second category must be considered in the $f\,(e_e)$ term of equation 7.12. The energy considered in the $f\,(e_e)$ term is a function of the amount of environmental energy available and the amount of effort required to change the environmental energy to a new value.

The energy available to an animal as a result of its performing work on the environment is a function of the amount of work expended, the manner in which the work is applied, and the nature of the environment. Figures 7.4 and 7.5 show the relationship between the direct energy of the animal and the availability of energy in the environment (nutrients and water). Let us consider the energy input to the animal as a function of the amount of work he performs and the availability of energy in the environment. If the environmental energy considered is in the form of nutrients, the general form of the energy relations will be shown in Figure 7-7. There is a family of curves which depend on the abundance of the nutrients and the work required for the animal to obtain the nutrients.

Curve A in Figure 7-7 results when there is an unlimited amount of nutrients in the environment, and they can be easily obtained by the animal with a small amount of work. Curve B results when the supply of nutrients are limited. As the nutrients become scarce, more work is required to obtain a given amount of nutrients. At some point, additional work will not increase the amount of nutrients available to the animal. Curve C represents a relatively severe environment as a large amount of work must be expended before any appreciable amount of energy is obtained from the environment. In addition, at some point, increasing work does not result in additional energy from the environment. Curve D represents the case of an extreme environment where an infinite amount of work by the animal would not yield energy output from the environment, e.g., outer space represents just such an environment for most animals.

There will be families of energy transfer curves for each animal species. A specific transfer curve can be obtained for a given animal species, a given set of environmental conditions, and a particular type of energy transformation, e.g., nutrients. These curves are plots of the transfer function $f(e_e)$ for various energy conditions. The function $f(e_e)$ represents the total energy transfer function between the work performed on the environment and the energy obtained from the environment as a result of this work. This function is the sum of many individual transfer function such as those for water, food, oxygen, etc. Symbolically, $f(e_e)$ can be expressed as:

$$f(e_e) = \sum_i f_i(e_e) \ , \ i = 1, 2, 3, \ldots \ldots \tag{7.14}$$

where $f_i(e_e)$ is the transfer function for the i-th variable.

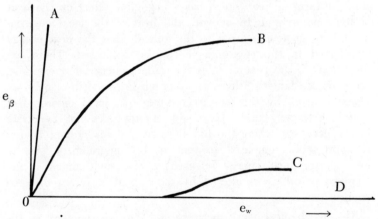

GENERALIZED TRANSFER FUNCTION FOR NUTRIENTS

Figure 7-7

191

A given animal species can change the function f_1 (e_e) over successive generations through better adaptation to the environment. In addition, certain animals have the capability of modifying their environment to some extent and therefore cause a modification of f (e_e).

The transfer functions developed in equation 7.12 and 7.13 are expressed in terms of the total energy output, $\int \dot{e}_w$ dt, of the animal. It was shown in Paragraph 7.3.2 that the total output energy of the animal can be expressed as a function of its constituent parts, i.e., mass, radiant, and mechanical energy as shown in equation 7.4. The mass energy $\int \dot{e}_{wm}$ dt is not involved in the transfer functions of equations 7.12 and 7.13, i.e., the mass leaving the animal does not perform work on the environment which results in environmental energy being available to the animal. In addition, we have seen previously that the atomic energy represented by this mass is not directed by the animal.

In general, the radiant energy from an animal $\int \dot{e}_{wh}$ dt does not perform work on the environment which will result in environmental energy being made available to the animal. For most animals, the radiant energy transferred to the environment is in the form of heat which has a negligible effect on the heat of the environment. In general, the heat of the local environment is so great compared to the animals that the heat energy transferred to the environment can be neglected. There are exceptions to the general rules for radiant energy. For example, the deep sea lantern fish emits radiation in the visible spectrum which is used by the fish to survive in a local environment that is extremely dark, i.e., light energy does not penetrate to the deep sea where the fish lives so that his radiant energy is appreciable compared to that of his environment. As, in general, the heat energy released to the environment is not changed or otherwise altered by the animal, it is not directed energy.

The mechanical work perform on the environment is the major agent for extracting energy from the environment and for converting animal energy into other forms of energy. Mechanical work is used in a broad sense herein and includes the chemical actions on the environment such as the excretion of enzymes to digest food in the environment, i.e., outside the body of the animal. Mechanical work also includes the energy expended in locomotion, gathering nutrients, ingesting nutrients, and moving environmental mass. When the mechanical energy is the major contributor in obtaining energy from the environment, equations 7.12 and 7.13 are simplified as the $\dot{e}_w$ term reduces to $\dot{e}_{ww}$.

When the energy available from the animal, which is involved in extracting energy from the environment, is considered to be in the form of mechanical energy, then equation 7.12 becomes:

$$\dot{e}_i = \dot{e}_\alpha + f(e_e)\dot{e}_{ww} \tag{7.15}$$

This energy input to the animal from the environment is either accepted by the animal or rejected in some manner, i.e.,

$$\dot{e}_i = \dot{e}_a + \dot{e}_r$$

The environmental energy flowing toward the animal through no effort on the part of the animal, i.e., $\dot{e}_\alpha$ can be considered as made up of a part which is subsequently accepted by the animal $\dot{e}_{\alpha a}$ and a part which is subsequently rejected by the animal $\dot{e}_{\alpha r}$ as follows:

$$\dot{e}_\alpha = \dot{e}_{\alpha a} + \dot{e}_{\alpha r} \tag{7.16}$$

It is possible that some of the energy obtained from the environment through the work process is subsequently rejected by the animal. However, it does not seem to me that rejected energy of this type will, in general, have a first order effect on the total rejected energy. Assuming that the rejected energy is of the form shown in equation 7.16, the energy input rate to the animal, as given by equation 7.15, becomes:

$$\dot{e} = \dot{e}_{\alpha a} + \dot{e}_{\alpha r} + f(e_e)\dot{e}_{ww} \tag{7.17}$$

193

Many animals have only the capability of operating on the environmental energy in a manner shown in equation 7.17, i.e., all the energy obtained from the environment is used as input energy to the animal. The directed environmental energy for these animals can be obtained by determining that energy in equation 7.17 which is directed by the animal. The impinging environmental energy accepted by the animal which is not the work by the animal, i.e., $\dot{e}_{\alpha a}$ is not directed by the animal while this energy is in the environment, hence it is not directed environmental energy. The environmental energy which is rejected by the animal, i.e., is operated on by the animal while the energy is at the animal — environment interface and therefore is directed environmental energy.

The energy obtained from the environment as a result of the animal working on the environment, i.e., $f(e_e) \dot{e}_{ww}$, is considered to be directed environmental energy. The directed environmental energy for animals whose total work energy output goes to obtain input energy for itself, based on the afore stated assumptions and considerations, can be expressed as:

$$\int \dot{e}_{d_e} dt = \int \left[\dot{e}_{\alpha r} + f(e_e) \dot{e}_{ww} \right] dt \qquad (7.18)$$

Certain animals have a capability for directing more environmental energy than that which is used solely as an input to themself, e.g., those which provide food for their offsprings have this capability. The method for obtaining this additional environmental energy is the process of performing work on the environment. Therefore, the additional energy is given by the term $f(e_e) \dot{e}_{ww}$ in equation 7.18. The additional energy is all directed environmental energy, therefore equation 7.18 is valid for this type animal. Certain homosapiens have the capability for directing more environmental energy than that required for their internal consumption and that of their offsprings. This additional directed energy can be expressed by equation 7.18, provided the function $f(e_e)$ is properly considered. Therefore, equation 7.18 is the basic directed environmental energy expression for all animals.

7.3.5 *Environmental Knowledge*

The environmental knowledge is equal to a constant multiplied by the total directed energy of the environment. It should be noted that energy from the environment which is transmitted through the substance without change is not considered as directed energy. The total environmental knowledge can be obtained from the directed environmental energy equation 7.18, as developed in the preceding paragraph.

The average environmental knowledge level at which an animal operates can be obtained by averaging the directed environmental energy over a sufficiently long period of time. For instance, some animals perform work in a short period of time but do not use the energy obtained from the environment until a much later time. Animals that gather food and store it for some later period provide examples of directed energy which must be considered over some time period. Indeed, some animals have the capability of storing energy to be used not by themselves but by a later generation. This stored energy is considered to be located in the environment until used by the animal.

7.3.6 *Total Animal Knowledge*

The total knowledge of an animal at time t is equal to the sum of internal, exchange, and environmental knowledge of the animal. In terms of directed energy, the total knowledge is equal to a constant times the sum of the directed energies as follows:

$$k = Se_d = S[e_{di} + e_{dw} + e_{de}] \tag{7.19}$$

where; e_{di} is the directed internal energy of the animal
$\quad\quad\quad e_{dw}$ is the exchange energy
$\quad\quad\quad e_{de}$ is the directed energy in the environment.

The directed internal, exchange, and environmental energies for an animal are given by equations 6.24, 7.7, and 7.18 respectively. Combining these equations obtains the total directed energy as follows:

$$e_d = m \int_{T_1}^{T_h} C \, dT + \sum_j M_j + \sum_k e_{fk} m_{ok} + F m_{Fs} +$$

$$\int \left(\sigma T^4 + KA \frac{dT}{dl} + \dot{\beta} \gamma_h e_F \right) dt +$$

$$\int \dot{\beta} \gamma_w e_F \, dt + \int \left[\dot{e}_{\alpha r} + f(\dot{e}_e) \dot{e}_{ww} \right] dt \qquad (7.20)$$

The total knowledge is obtained by multiplying the directed energy, as given by equation 7.20, by the appropriate constant. For the basic knowledge unit established in this book, this constant is equal to one.

If the animal is in energy equilibrium with the environment, i.e., steady state, the internal energy of the animal, the directed energy in the environment, the input and the output energy rates are constant. Under these steady state conditions, the total knowledge of the animal is constant. A mature animal of constant weight on a steady regime of diet and work, and who does not store food or other energy for use at a later time is approximately in a steady state condition. The maximum total knowledge, i.e., maximum capability, is obtained by using maximum directed energy capabilities in equation 7.20. For instance, the maximum knowledge capability would be a condition where the energy input to the animal is as large as it can be consistent with the physical limitations of the animal, the energy output is the maximum work capability of the animal, the internal energy is the maximum amount the animal can have and still function normally, and environmental energy is being directed consistent with the maximum work output exerted on the environment.

A functional diagram for an animal-environment energy system is much the same as that for plants, the difference being in the expression for the environmental energy function. The functional relations for the environment are different from that of plants in order to account for the capabilities of an animal to direct certain environmental energies. The relationship for the energy in an animal's environment is given by equation 7.17. A functional diagram of an animal-environment system is given in Figure 7-8.

A functional diagram of an animal's directed energy is shown in figure 7-9. This diagram is based on the directed energy of an animal as developed in the preceding paragraphs.

*7.4 Example of Animal Knowledge

An example of a "higher form" of animal life is given to demonstrate basic principles. Man is used for the animal knowledge example. Man does not represent the animal with the largest organizational, i.e. internal, knowledge as this type knowledge is primarily a function of the size of the animal and obviously man is not the largest animal on earth. In addition, man does not have the largest exchange knowledge as this type knowledge is a function of the energy transferred between the environment and the animal which again is primarily related to the size of the animal. However, man does seem to have more knowledge related to the direction of environmental energy.

Man was selected as an example as he is of major concern to most of us, a large body of information exists about man, and he is generally considered, within the current popular concept of knowledge, to be the only animal with "knowledge" or at least the most "knowledgeable" animal to exist or to ever have existed.

*7.4.1 Essential Characteristics

The general characteristics of animals are given in Paragraph 7.1. In the frame of reference of these general characteristics, man is a highly developed multi-cellular animal having well developed tissue and organs, is warm blooded, and can metabolize a wide range of nutrients. The following detail characteristics of man are necessary for our example.

Mass.   The mass of man, as for all plants and animals, is important in the determination of his organizational energy and knowledge. The mass of man varies as a function of his growth period, race, nutrients, and other factors. The change in mass during the growth period can be observed almost on

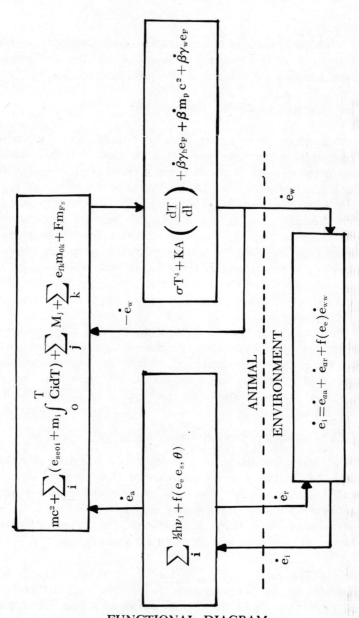

FUNCTIONAL DIAGRAM

ANIMAL SYSTEM ENERGY

Figure 7-8

198

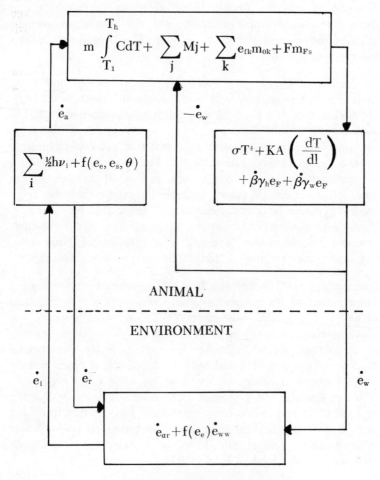

FUNCTIONAL DIAGRAM

ANIMAL SYSTEM DIRECTED ENERGY

Figure 7-9

199

a daily basis in our children. The variation in mass with race is a well established fact. The pygmy of central Africa is an example of a race of dwarf people of small mass. There are races of people that have a larger average mass than the norm for the human species. The mass of the human species is also a function of sex; the female being generally smaller than the male. For purposes of illustration, we will assume an average mass of the man in our example to be 70 kilograms (approximately 155 pounds).

Temperature. The human species is warm blooded and must maintain its temperature within narrow limits. Changes in body temperature of less than 10 percent from the normal temperature usually results in death. If the temperature of the local environment increases to such an extent that the cooling process of the body cannot maintain the body temperature within allowable limits, then death occurs. If the temperature of the local environment decreases to such an extent that the body cannot generate heat as rapidly as it is being lost by the body, then death occurs. The absolute temperature of the local environment which results in death is a function of body area, sex, race, and degree of adaptation to the environment.

Specific Heat. The specific heat of an animal depends to a large extent on its composition, particulary upon its percentage of water. The specific heat of several animals which are human food products, are given in Reference 7.5. Oysters, with a water contenant of 80.38 percent have an above freezing specific heat of 0.84 whereas fat pork with a water content of 39 percent has an above freezing specific heat of 0.51. Lean beef with a water content of 72 percent has an above freezing specific heat of 0.77. The below freezing specific heat of this lean beef is 0.41. The specific heat of man will also depend on his water content and the temperature. It will be assumed for this example that the specific heat of man is 0.75.

Metabolism. Man requires oxygen, water, and nutrient to carry out his metabolic processes. Man can metabolize carbohydrates, fat and protein. The rate of metabolism is a function of surface area, age, sex, work output, climate, race and seasonal variations. (Reference 7.1).

The heat production, during rest, of animals such as the horse, dog, rabbit, mouse and fowl is dependent on their surface area (Voit - Reference 7.6). The heat output of these animals and man is approximately 1000 calories* per square meter per day. A law was postulated by Rubner (7.7) that metabolism is proportional to the superficial area of an animal. The average heat output for the normal male between the ages of 20 and 40 years is 39.5 calories per square meter per hour. Normal females in this age group have an average heat output of 36.5 - 37 calories per square meter per hour.

The surface area of the human species may be calculated by the following formula proposed by D. DuBois and E. F. DuBois (Reference 7.8):

$$A = W^{0.425} \times H^{0.725} \times 71.84$$

Where A = area in square centimeters, W = weight in kilograms, and H = height in centimeters.

The caloric requirements of man is a function of the factors mentioned above. When the caloric intake and caloric output are equal, man is in caloric equilibrium: which is the normal state of the adult individual. The basal metabolism of an adult weighing 70 kg is aproximately 1750 calories for a 24 hour period. This value increases for the slightest activity. The process of food ingestion increases the basal metabolism by 10 to 12 percent (Reference 7.1). Physical work is the major factor which affects the metabolic rate. It has been shown by Becker and Hamalainen (Reference 7.9) that the energy requirements, for men in Finland, vary from 2400 calories in 24 hours for tailors to 5400 calories in 24 hours for men sawing wood. In the same study, it was determined that the requirement for women varied from 1800 calories per 24 hours for seamstress (needle) to 3400 calories per 24 hours for washerwomen. As stated previously, the energy transfer function of man is a function of the type of nutrients that are metabolized. In

*Note: In this chapter, unless specified otherwise, the term "calorie" will be used in referring to the large or kilogram calorie.

addition, there are metabolic differences inherent in a given individual due to surface area, age, sex, race, etc.

Energy Transfer. Man accepts energy from the environment in the form of nutrients (food), water, oxygen, radiant energy and mechnical energy. The nutrients and water are accepted by ingestion. Oxygen is accepted by the respiratory system. The radiant energy is accepted by the skin over the superficial area of the body. The radiant energy can be in the complete frequency spectrum. The amount of energy accepted at a given frequency is a function of the intensity of the energy and the characteristics of the skin. The skin has selective absorption properties, i.e., it will accept radiant energy more readily at one frequency than at another. Man can accept mechanical energy from the environment, generally in the form of heat due to the transfer of energy from the atmospheric environment by the process of air molecules colliding with the body (conduction heating). Man can also accept mechanical energy from the environment in the form of a velocity with respect to the environment. A man floating down stream in a river is an example of his accepting mechanical energy from the environment.

Man releases energy to the environment in the form of mass (excreta), water, carbon dioxide, radiant energy and mechanical energy. Mass can be released to the environment in the form of feces, urine, perspiration, and gas. The amount of mass released as feces varies greatly with diet and other factors. The average amount is about 200 grams in a 24 hour period but may be much larger when a vegetable diet is being used (Reference 7.10). The amount of mass released in the form of urine varies greatly with the amount of liquids ingested, perspiration, etc. The average amount of urine voided by a normal adult in the United States is about 40 to 50 ounces (1200 to 1500 CC) (Reference 7.10). The amount of mass released by perspiration varies over such a wide range as a function of work performed, climatic conditions, local heat environment, etc., that an average amount does not have meaning. The amount of mass released to the environment in the form of carbon dioxide varies greatly as a function of the amount and type of food ingested, the work performed, and other factors. The amount of carbon dioxide can be determined by the metabolic equations, the amount and type of metabolites and the respiratory quotients. The release of heat energy from the body to the environment is in the form of radiation and mechanical energy. The processes of releasing heat are:

- radiation
- conduction and convection
- warming the inspired air (conduction)
- excreta (feces, urine, and CO_2 are warm)
- evaporation of water from lungs and skin.

The release of heat is a function of body area and moistness of the surface, time of exposure, temperature gradient between the surface and the local atmosphere, humidity of the atmosphere, and the wind intensity. According to Hardy (7.11) the skin radiates like a black body irrespective of the visible color of the skin. Burns (7.12) has given a rough estimate of the loss of heat in a 24 hour period as 2470 calories. Of this total, 73% was released by radiation and conduction, 21.7% by evaporation (14.5% by skin), 5.3% by excreta (about 3.5% by CO_2). The amount of mechanical energy a man can release to the environment is a function of the size of the individual, his training, diet and other factors. It has been estimated that the maximum gross efficiency of man performing muscular work, such as pulling a heavy load, is approximately 25 percent. The gross efficiency of muscular work being defined by the following formula (Brody and Cunningham, Reference 7.13).

$$\text{Gross efficiency} = \frac{\text{energy equivalent of mechanical work accomplished}}{\text{total energy expended while accomplishing work}}$$

For example, if 100 calories of total energy is expended during hard work, a maximum of 25 calories may be recovered as work accomplished. The remaining 75 calories is used for basal metabolism, heat increment of feeding, standing above basal, walking with load above standing, overcoming internal resistance of the body, useless incidental movements, etc.

Extraction of Energy from the Environment. Man extracts energy from the environment. Man is not unique in this respect as many animals perform work on the environment to extract energy. Man has the capability of performing work on the environment and storing energy in the environment for use at some later time. Again man is not unique in this respect, e.g., other animals, such as the squirrel, have the capability of storing food in the form of nuts for use at a later time. Man has the capability of using simple tools such as levers to amplify the amount of force that can be exerted on the environment. Here again, man is not unique as the monkey can perform certain of the same functions. Man can build structures to store energy in the environment. The beaver also has this capability. It is the extent to which man can direct environmental energy which sets him somewhat apart from other animals. The amount of environmental energy that can be directed by man is a function of the local environment and the amount of knowledge possessed by his particular race, tribe, clan, or social order. There are tribes of man on earth today that do not have the capability to store environmental energy. Certain primitive nomad tribes are examples of this type of man. In general, many of the nomad tribes and the tribes living in a benevolent environment do not have or have only a limited capability of storing environmental energy or directing environmental energy greater than that required for basic body maintenance.

Western man has developed a capability for directing large amounts of environmental energy at his convenience. Electrical power and atomic power are examples of large amounts of directed environmental energy. Based on the preceding argument, it is seen that there cannot be an "average" or "normal" amount of directed environmental energy for all of mankind. It is only proper to discuss the methods of calculating this directed energy and the factors which influence the capability to direct environmental energy or to discuss a specific man in a given local environment.

°7.4.2 *Knowledge of Man*

An adult man in his "normal" environment is used for example purposes. Therefore, the knowledge calculated in the example represent the knowledge level at which man normally operates and does not provide a measure of man's maximum knowledge capability. The essential characteristics of this "normal" or "ideal" man are given in Paragraph 7.4.1.

Internal Knowledge

The normal internal knowledge of man is obtained by evaluating the internal directed energy equation (6.24) under the proper set of conditions. The first term in equation 6.24, i.e., the internal heat, is evaluated for an "ideal" man with a mass of 70 kilograms and a specific heat of 0.75 calories per gram per degree centigrade. The upper limit on the integral is the normal temperature of man, i.e., 37.5 degrees centigrade. The lower limit of integration is assumed to be 16 degree centigrade. This latter assumption is based on the fact that cats are unable to survive when their rectal temperature falls below 16° C, Reference 7.14. Experimental data on the temperature at which a man dies is rather sparse, therefore the low temperature is assumed based on the data for cats. The directed heat energy becomes:

$$m \int_{16}^{37.5} C\, dT = 70 \times 10^3 \int_{16}^{37.5} 0.75\, dT$$
$$= (70 \times 10^3)\,(0.75)\,(21.5) = 1.13 \times 10^6 \text{ small cal.}$$
$$= 4.74 \times 10^6 \text{ Joules.}$$

The term Fm_{Fs} of the directed internal energy equation is an expression for the stored internal energy. For purpose of illustration, it is assumed that the "ideal" man has 10 pounds of stored internal energy in the form of fat. The usable energy in a gram of fat is usually taken to be 9 calories per gram (Reference 6.14). The directed internal stored energy, under these assumptions, is:

$$Fm_{Fs} = (9\,\text{Kg cal/g})\,(10\,\text{lbs})\,(453.6\,\text{g/lb})$$
$$= 4.09 \times 10^7 \text{ small calories}$$
$$= 1.71 \times 10^8 \text{ Joules.}$$

The miscellaneous energy term in the internal directed energy equation, namely $\sum_{j} M_j$ accounts for all the miscellaneous and incidental directed energy in an animal. For man, these include the flow of fluids such as blood, urine, sweat; energies due to various body movements, etc. The body fluids flow rather slowly, resulting in relatively low energies when compared to the stored energies and heat energies. As the purpose of the example is to show application of theory and not to give precise calculations, the miscellaneous and incidental energies are neglected.

Assuming that the organizational energy per unit mass is 6 kilogram calories per gram of mass and that the basic organizational mass is 65.5 kilograms, i.e., 70 kilograms less the assumed internal stored food in the form of fat (10 pounds or 4.5 kilograms), then the organizational energy is:

$$(6 \times 10^3)\ (65.5 \times 10^3)\ (4.186)$$
$$= 1.64 \times 10^9 \text{ Joules.}$$

For the assumptions and conditions of the internal directed energy calculations, the total internal directed energy of our "ideal" man is approximately 1.82×10^9 Joules. The internal knowledge of our "Ideal" man, under the stated conditions, is equal to approximately 1.82×10^9 knowledge units.

Exchange Knowledge

The exchange knowledge for man, as for other substances, is based on the direction of the energy which passes through the substance from the environment. This energy conversion is shown in simple schematic form as follows:

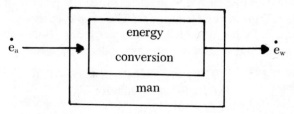

It was shown that the amount of exchange energy directed can be expressed as:

$$e_{dw} = \int [\sigma T^4 + KA \frac{dT}{dl} + \dot{\beta}\gamma_h e_F] dt + \int \dot{\beta}\gamma_w e_F dt$$

where the first integral term of the equation is a function of the heat released to the environment and the second integral term is a function of the work performed on the environment.

To evaluate the heat term, it is necessary to know the area of our "ideal" man. Let us assume that our ideal man weighs 70 kilograms and is 173 centimeters high (five feet eight inches). Then by the DuBois formula, the superficial body area is:

$$A = 70^{0.425} \times 173^{0.725} \times 71.84$$
$$= 1.84 \times 10^4 \text{ cm}^2.$$

It is assumed that the first two terms in the heat expression, i.e., heat radiation and conduction, are to be evaluated for ambient temperature conditions. That is, it is assumed that the man transmits heat energy from an earth ambient temperature into an absolute zero degree environment. In terms of accepted energy, the assumption means that the energy to maintain the body at an earth ambient temperature must come from the environment. The last term in the heat expression is due to metabolism.

The radiant energy term, under the stated assumptions, is:

$$\sigma T^4 = (5.672 \times 10^{-5} \text{ ergs/cm}^2/\text{deg}^4/\text{sec}) \; (1.84 \times 10^4 \text{ cm}^2) \; (290°)^4$$
$$= (1.04) \; (7.08 \times 10^9) = 7.37 \times 10^9 \text{ ergs/second}$$
$$= 7.37 \times 10^2 \text{ Joules/second.}$$

To obtain an insight into the effect of thermal conduction, it is necessary to make certain assumptions about the nature of the ideal man's environment· As we are trying to obtain an estimate of the heat energy which is flowing through the man, it is necessary to determine the heat energy which would be conducted into a zero degree temperature environment from a man at ambient temperature. It is assumed that the man is surrounded by an air layer which is 30.5 centimeters thick (approximately one foot) and that the outside of the air layer is at absolute zero degrees temperature. Under these assumptions, the heat energy conducted from the man is:

$$KA\frac{dT}{dl} = (5.68\times10^{-5})(1.84\times10^{4})\left(\frac{290}{30}\right)$$

$$= (1.04)(9.68) = 10.1 \text{ calories/second}$$
$$= 42 \text{ Joules/second.}$$

Rather than trying to calculate the metabolic heat transfer term, measured data is used. Burns (Reference 7.12) determined that the heat energy released to the environment under conditions of no work and in an ambient temperature environment is 2470 calories in a 24 hour period. This is equivalent to 28.6 small calories per second or 1.19×10^{2} Joules per second. Therefore the metabolic heat transfer rate or our ideal man is:

$$\dot{\beta}\gamma_{h}e_{F} = 1.19\times10^{2} \text{ Joules/second.}$$

Under the stated assumptions, the heat energy transfer rate to the environment becomes:

$$\sigma T^{4} + KA\frac{dT}{dl} + \dot{\beta}\gamma_{h}e_{F} = 7.37\times10^{2} + 4.2\times10^{1} + 1.19\times10^{2}$$

$$= 898 \text{ Joules/second.}$$

The work energy, as represented by the last term in the directed exchange energy equation, is determined based on experimental data rather than evaluating the work term. It is assumed that the ideal man is expending 2470 calories of heat energy and that while expending this energy, he is expending 822 calories in work. That is, he is expending a total of 3292 calories per day and approximately 25 percent of this expenditure is in the form of work performed on the environment. The average rate of work is 9.5 small calories per second or 39.8 Joules per second. That is:

$$\dot{\beta}\gamma_{w}e_{F} = 39.8 \text{ Joules/second.}$$

The total directed energy is the sum of the heat and the work energy rate, i.e., 938 Joules per second.

The total energy operated on by the ideal man as it passes from the environment through the man and on to the environment during the standard one second time interval is:

$$e_{dw} = \int_0^1 (9.38 \times 10^2 \text{ Joules/sec}) \, dt = 938 \text{ Joules.}$$

The exchange knowledge level associated with this energy is 938 knowledge units.

Environmental Knowledge

The environment energy directed by a particular man is obtained by evaluating equation 7.18. The environmental knowledge is then obtained from the directed environmental energy. The first term in equation 7.18, i.e., the rejected energy, is reasonable constant for most men. The rejected energy can, of course, be changed by the simple expedient of donning clothes. However the basic radiant energy rejection of the unclothed body is similar for most men. For purposes of the example, the energy rejected at the surface of the body is assumed to be in the form of solar radiation. Other surface effects such as wind are assumed to be negligible· To determine the rejected solar energy, we need to know the area of the body, the solar energy falling on the body and the percent of incident energy that is rejected at the surface. Let us again assume that our "ideal" man weighs 70 kgrams and is 173 cm high (five feet eight inches). Then by the DuBois formula, the superficial body area is $1.84 \times 10^4 \text{ cm}^2$ as calculated previously.

The solar radiation constant near the earth is 1.92 gram calories (small) per minute falling on one square centimeter or .032 gram calories per sec. on one square centimeter. Let us assume a maximum rejected energy case where the body area exposed to radiant solar energy is ½A, the full solar radiation impinges on the body for 12 hours per day and the coefficient of reflection is one. Then the average rate of energy rejection is:

$$\dot{e}_{\alpha r} = \text{½} \ (1.84 \times 10^4) \ \times \ (0.032) \ (\text{½}) = 1.47 \times 10^2 \text{g calories/sec.}$$
$$= 6.15 \times 10^2 \text{ Joules/second.}$$

Under normal conditions of shade from clouds, foliage, etc., and more realistic values of radiated area, the value of $\dot{e}_{\alpha r}$ will be greatly reduced.

The concept of a "normal" environment and an "ideal" man

is not directly applicable to environmental knowledge. The capacity for directing environmental energy varies over a wide range from one society of man to another. In addition, small changes in the local environment can cause great changes in normal directed energy. Therefore, to determine environmental knowledge levels we must completely specify the environment and the particular man of interest.

For purposes of illustration, let us choose a few representative local environments and a few men in differing social orders. First, let us choose a benevolent environment such as a geographic area in the equatorial belt where there is an abundant food supply. It requires very little energy to survive in an environment such as this. The temperature is always sufficiently high that directed energy in the form of fire or shelter is not required. The food supply is abundant all year so that food storage is not required. In this postulated environment, a man needs to direct energy only to obtain his daily food supply. From the essential characteristics of man, we have that approximately 2000 calories are required just for basal metabolism and food digestion. The energy expended to gather food in an environment with an abundant food supply should not be greater than 400 calories for a total daily expenditure of 2400 calories. This amount of energy is expended by a tailor in Finland (see essential characteristics) which should be approximately the same amount as that required for a food gathering man. From the transfer function point of view (Figure 7-7), 400 calories of mechanical work will allow the man to gather sufficient food to supply 2400 calories of energy from the environment. For a simple food gathering man, the actual work on the environment will be less than his work output due to inefficient work methods. If energy can be obtained from the environment rather easily, then one would expect the energy obtained from the environment to increase approximately linearly as the man performed more work. The transfer function for this postulated condition can be represented as shown in Figure 7-10.

The transfer function shown in Figure 7-10 is based on the assumption that the man uses his own native capacity to perform work and does not use tools of any kind. If the man

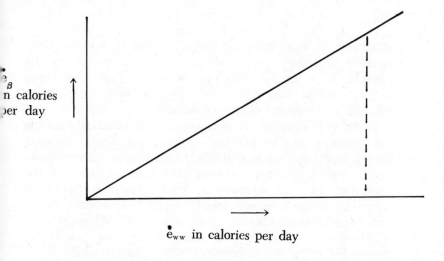

$\overset{\bullet}{B}$
n calories
per day

$\overset{\bullet}{e}_{ww}$ in calories per day

Figure 7-10

has the capability to use tools, the slope of the curve increases and he is able to obtain more energy from the environment for the same amount of expended energy. The better his tools, the steeper the slope of the curve. The introduction of tools could cause the curve in Figure 7.10 to be non linear. For instance, a given amount of mechanical energy may be required before a tool becomes effective and at that time a steep increase in the energy output from the environment may result. That is, the curve may be discontinuous at the point where the tool becomes effective.

Let us assume an environment such as the one stipulated above, with the exception that the food supply is limited. The transfer function can be of the form shown by curve B in Figure 7-7. Let us also assume a very primitive man that does not have tools and obtains his food by gathering. If the local environment contains sufficient food for the primitive man to just live, provided he works at his maximum capacity, then we would expect a transfer curve some what as given in Figure 7-11. This figure is not intended to be precise or even completely representative, as the exact shape of the curve cannot be determined without further specifying the environ-

211

ment and the food gathering process. If the food in the environment becomes easier to obtain, the upper portion of the curve shifts to the left. This may be due to more food being available in the environment or the man learns to be more efficient in the food gathering process.

If the local environment does not contain sufficient food for our primitive man, he becomes a nomad and obtains his food from a larger environment. If our primitive man learns to grow his own food then he has been able to direct more of the energy of the local environment. That is, he now directs, to some extent, those environmental energies which make things grow such as solar radiation, earth minerals, etc. When primitive man learns to grow foods he makes a large increase in his knowledge as he can direct much more environmental energy. Man can grow food without the aid of specialized tools; however, when man uses tools in the growing of food, he has the capacity to direct even more environmental energy. From the viewpoint of our transfer function, learning to grow food and the use of agricultural tools change the scale of the ordinate in Figure 7-11. The new scale of the ordinate axis can be determined only

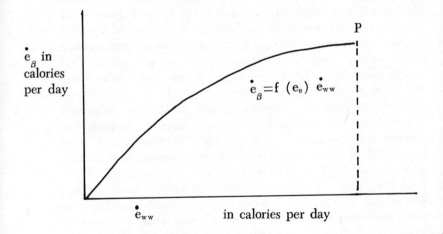

Figure 7-11

upon the complete specification of the environment, the particular man, and his tools.

As man finds ways to direct more of the energy of the environment, he can live in the environments which were uninhabitable for him prior to his discoveries, he can live in the same environment with less expenditure of his work on the environment, or he can adjust his local environment to better suit his desires. Some societies of man have learned to exist for periods of time in hostile environments such as the sea and outer space. These feats require the direction and storage of large amounts of environmental energy.

Certain societies of man have found many ways to direct environmental energy. The major discoveries such as agricultural methods, mechanical laws of physics, electricity, communication, transportation, atomic energy, etc., are all manifestations of man's ability to direct the environmental energy. Causing another person to expend energy by relaying a command over a communication system is a method of directing environmental energy. If the communication system did not exist, the man expends his energy traveling to the person to be directed. With a communication system, he expends very little of his energy to direct the same amount of energy from the other person. In particular, if we consider all remote control to be in the purview of communications, the direction of energy through a communication system is easily seen.

Transportation is also a tool for directing energy. If man rides an animal between two points, he has transported himself over the distance with very little expenditure of his energy. However, he has extracted the amount of energy to transport himself over the distance from the animal; the animal being considered as part of the environment. The applicability to other modes of transportation is readily apparent.

Discovery in the fields of atomic physics, electricity, and mechanics have provided laws and devices and methods for directing environmental energy.

Let us now specify an environment and a man of a given social order. Based on this specification, we will calculate the directed environmental energy and the environmental knowledge. Again, no claim is made for the exactness of the numerical example; the purpose of the example is only to demonstrate methods. The environment is specified as the equatorial belt or the lower latitudes of the temperate zone, just sufficient food for the man, and the food rather difficult to obtain, requiring the full energy output of the man. The man is specified as a very primitive one. He does not have tools and is not capable of storing food in the environment. He has the capability of expending 8000 calories per 24 hours when performing work at his maximum rate. Let us assume that 25 percent of the energy above his base level of 2000 calories is in the form of mechanical work, i.e., 1500 calories per 24 hours. This assumption simplifies the calculations and still serves our purpose of illustrating principles. Let it be further assumed that the man is 60 percent efficient in the actual performance of work on the environment. That is, only 60 percent of his actual work output is properly applied to the environment to obtain food. Then 900 calories per 24 hours are considered to be directed environmental energy. This is equivalent to 10.4 small calories per second or 43.5 Joules per second.

Let it be assumed that the total effective work output is required to obtain the 8000 calories from the environment. Under the stated conditions, the 8000 calories are directed energy. Converting this energy to small calories per second obtains 92.5 small calories/second or 386 Joules/second.

The environmental knowledge level of the primitive man, under the very restrictive conditions of the example, is the sum of the rejected and the work energy. This sum is 1044 Joules per second. Using the standard time interval and the knowledge relationship obtains an environmental knowledge of 1044 knowledge units.

Knowledge of Primitive Man

In summary, we have that the primitive man in the stipulated environment has the following knowledge:

• internal	1.82×10^9 knowledge units
• exchange	9.38×10^2	,,	,,
• environmental	$\underline{10.44 \times 10^2}$	,,	,,
TOTAL	1.82×10^9	,,	,,

Due to the restrictive nature of the example, conclusions should not be inferred from these numerical values.

Chapter VIII

EPILOGUE

8.0 *Introduction*

In this concluding chapter, the kernel of the theory is summarized and the basic equations restated. In addition, thoughts are presented on the possible application and utility of the theory·

8.1 *Essence of the Theory of Knowledge*

The theory of knowledge which has been presented herein provides a basis for obtaining a quantitative measure of the knowledge of all substances. That is, it provides a measure of knowledge. The theory is essentially embodied in the statement;

> An individual's knowledge is directly proportional to its capacity to direct energy

This basic statement can be expressed more precisely as:

> An individual's knowledge (k) is directly proportional to the amount of energy (e_d) it can direct, this directed energy having a lower boundary of zero and an upper boundary of e_T, where e_T is the total energy in a system consisting of the individual and its environment, i.e.,

$$k = Se_d \qquad\qquad 0 \leqq e_d \leqq e_T$$

The theory provides for the determination of the total knowledge of an individual, i.e., the total energy directing capacity, and for the knowledge used for a given set of cricumstances, i.e., the energy directed by an individual under a given set of circumstances.

To express knowledge quantitatively, a unit of measure is required. The unit of measure selected is the knowledge unit which is defined as follows:

> One unit of knowledge results when a substance directs one Joule of energy. For this unit of measure, the constant (S) in the knowledge equaiton is set equal to one. The fundamental knowledge equation becomes;
>
> $$k = e_d \text{ knowledge units} \qquad\qquad 0 \leqq e_d \leqq e_T$$

When e_d is expressed in Joules, the constant S has a unit of $(\text{Joules})^{-1}$ in this unit system for knowledge. Other units of knowledge could have been selected based on larger or smaller energy units, however the unit based on the Joule will probably have the most all around utility.

8.2 Basic Relations for Substances

It has been shown in this book that the theory of knowledge measure applies to all substances, i.e., animal, plant, and mineral. Equations have been developed which relate directed energy, hence knowledge, to the characteristics of the substance. The development proceeded from the most simple mineral individual to the most sophisticated animal individual. The directed energy of a substance can be considered as the sum of the directed energy internal to the substance, the energy flow between the substance and the environment which is directed by the substance, and the energy in the environment that is directed by the substance. The energy directed by a sophisticated animal can be expressed by the generalized equation:

$$e_d = m \int_{T_1}^{T_h} C \, dT + \sum_j M_j + \sum_k e_{fk}m_{ok} + Fm_{Fs} +$$

$$\int \left(\sigma T^4 + KA \frac{dT}{dl} + \dot\beta \gamma_h e_F\right) dt +$$

$$\int \dot\beta \gamma_w e_F \, dt + \int [\dot e_{\alpha r} + f(\dot e_e) \dot e_{ww}] dt$$

The directed energy of a less sophisticated substance can be obtained by deleting the proper terms from this general equation.

The energy directed by a plant can be expressed by the generalized equation:

$$e_d = m \int_{T_1}^{T_h} C \, dT + \sum_j M_j + \sum_k e_{fk}m_{ok} + Fm_{Fs} +$$

$$\int \left(\sigma T^4 + KA \frac{dT}{dl} + \dot\beta \gamma_h e_F\right) dt + \int e_{\alpha r} \, dt$$

The directed energy of a mineral individual, i.e. a molecule, is given by the equation:

$$e_d = m \int_{T_1}^{T_h} C \, dT + \int \left(\sigma T^4 + KA \frac{dT}{dl}\right) dt + \int e_{\alpha r} \, dt.$$

8.3 *Semantic Problem*

The concept that a mineral can direct energy and therefore has knowledge seems to present a semantic problem for some people. The difficulty is caused by the notion that to direct, control, or operate upon something implies a willed phenomenon to many people. Directing energy is not necessarily a willed phenomenon; e.g., the sun directs energy toward the earth and this directed energy is not willed by man or by a willing process of the sun. When the energy from the sun strikes the earth it is redirected, but not by a willed process. Man also directs energy that is not willed by him, e.g. certain environ-

219

mental energy impinges on man, such as heat and solar energy, which is redirected by man; man can will to his heart's content but not change his body's capability to redirect this energy.

When it is recognized that directed energy is not necessarily willed, the concept of knowledge and directed energy is easily seen to apply to all substances in the universe. It is rather gratifying to see from the examples that a man has many orders of magnitude more knowledge than a mineral individual. It is also rather satisfying to the ego to observe that a man has organizational, i.e. internal, knowledge and exchange knowledge that is exceeded only by a few animals, and that man in advanced societies has more environmental knowledge than all other animals.

8.4   Utility of Knowledge Theory

To be meaningful, a theory which allows the measurement of knowledge should have some utility. Some of the possible uses of· the theory of knowledge developed in this book are discussed in the following paragraphs.

Classification

The theory of knowledge provides a method of classifying all substances in the universe. It was shown in the development of knowledge theory that all substances have knowledge. Indeed, it was stated that when energy takes form, it assumes the attribute of knowledge. Therefore, all substances can be categorized by the amount of knowledge they possess. Substances can be classified further by type of knowledge, i. e., organizational, exchange, and environmental. As science starts with classification, the classification of substances by their knowledge forms the foundation of any science based on the attribute of knowledge.

Adaptation

The measure of a substance's knowledge provides an indication of its ability to fit into or adjust to its environment. The knowledge capacity of a substante allows the prediction of the ability of a substance to cope with or adapt to a changing environment.

Social Science

The social sciences have a common basis in the knowledge of man. All are dependent to some degree on the capacity of man to direct the energy in his environment or to direct his own energy. Even a social theorem as basic as the Malthusian theorem on population, i. e., the population increases in a geometric progression while the food supply increases in an arithemetic progression, is modified by knowledge. As a matter of fact, one of the major reasons for the current controversy on the theorem is that it fails to account for knowledge. If man's knowledge was injected into the Malthus theorem, it is seen that the increase in population would be modified by controlling the number of people and hence the total organizational knowledge of groups of people. In addition, as man increases his ability to obtain food, the rate of increasing food changes from an arithmetic progression.

I feel that the greatest potential for a theory of knowledge measure lies in the field of the behavioral and social sciences.

REFERENCES

1.1   Bohr, Niels, Atomic Physics and Human Knowledge, Science Editions, Inc., New York, 1961.

1.2   Ashby, W. R. Principles of the Self-Organizing Systems, Principles of Self-Organization, Von Foester, H. and Zopf, G., Eds·, Pergamon Press, New York, 1961.

1.3   Shannon, C. E., and McCarthy, (Eds.) Automata Studies, Princeton University Press, 1956.

1.4   Minsky, M. L., Hueristic Aspects of the Artificial Intelligence Problem, Group Report 34-55, Lincoln Laboratory, Massachusetts Institute of Technology, 17 December 1956·

1.5   Getzels, J. W., and Jackson, P. W., Creativity and Intelligence, John Wiley and Sons, Inc. New York, 1962.

3.1   Richtmyer, F. K. and Kennard E. H., Introduction to Modern Physics, McGraw-Hill Book Company. Inc. 1947, Paragraph 155.

3.2   Prutton, C. F., and Maron, S. H., Fundamental Principles of Physical Chemistry, The Macmillan Company, New York, 1947, Chapter XXII.

3.3   Goldman, Stanford, Information Theory, Prentice-Hall Inc., 1954.

3.4   Schrödinger, Erwin, What is Life? The Physical Aspects of the Living Cell. University Press, Cambridge, 1944.

3.5   Lwoff, André, Biological Order, The MIT Press, Massachusetts Institute of Technology, Cambridge Massachusetts, 1965.

3.6   Brillouin, L., Science and Information Theory. Academic Press, New York, 1956.

4.1   Handbook of Chemistry and Physics, 30th Edition.

4.2   Hausmann, E., and Slack, E. P., Physics, D. Van Nostrand Company, Inc. Second Edition, Chapter XVI.

4.3   Encyclopaedia Britannica, 1951, Volume 7, pages 830 to 837.

5.1 Cork, J. M., Heat, John Wiley and Son, Inc., 1947, Chapter IV.

5.2 Prutton, C. F. and Maron, S. H., Fundamental Principles of Physical Chemistry, The Macmillan Company, New York, 1947, Chapter XXII.

5.3 Richtmyer, F. K. and Kennard, E. H., Introduction to Modern Physics, McGraw-Hill Book Company, 1947, page 162.

5.4 Cork, J. M., Heat, John Wiley and Son Inc., 1947, page 51.

5.5 Cork, J. M., Heat, John Wiley and Son Inc., 1947, page 143.

6.1 Encyclopaedia Britannica, 1951, Volume 6, page 941.

6.2 Encyclopaedia Britannica, 1951, Volume 3, page 592.

6.3 Encyclopaedia Britannica, 1951, Volume 3, page 593.

6.4 Mac Dougall, M. S., Hegner, R., Biology the Science of Life, McGraw-Hill Book Company, Inc., 1943, page 575.

6.5 Ferry, James F., and Ward, Henry S., Fundamentals of Plant Physiology, The Macmillan Company, New York, 1959.

6.6 Bodansky, M., Introduction to Physiological Chemistry, John Wiley and Son, Inc. 1938, page 519.

6.7 Todd, J. C., Sandford, A. H., and Wells, B. B., Clinical Diagnosis by Laboratory Methods, Saunders, 1953.

6.8 Encyclopaedia Britannica, 1951, Volume 3, page 598 A.

6.9 Encyclopaedia Britannica, 1951, Volume 2, page 903.

6.10 Menzel, D. H., Fundamental Formulas of Physics, Volume II, Chapter 13 Biophysics, Dover Publications, Inc. 1960.

6.11 Encyclopaedia Britannica, 1951, Volume 18, page 25.

6.12 Bodansky, Meyer, Introduction to Physiological Chemistry, Fourth Edition, John Wiley and Son, Inc. 1938, page 519.

6.13 Fry, Walter and White, John, R., Big Trees, Stanford University Press, 1938.

6.14 Bodansky, Meyer, Introduction to Physiological Chemistry, Fourth Edition, John Wiley and Son, Inc., 1938.

6.15 Encyclopaedia Britannica, 1951, Volume 18, page 19.

6.16 Rogers, Julie Ellen, Trees Worth Knowing, Little Nature Library, Nelson Doubleday, 1924.

6.17   Cook, Lawrence, F., The Giant Sequoias of California, U.S. Government Printing Office Pamplet 1961, Reprint.

6.18   Encyclopaedia Britannica, 1951, Volume 18, page 21.

6.19   Encyclopaedia Britannica, 1951, Volume 18, page 23.

7.1   Bodansky, Meyer, Introduction to Physiological Chemistry, Fourth Edition, John Wiley and Son, Inc., 1938.

7.2   Mac Dougall, M. S., Hegner, R., Biology the Science of Life, McGraw-Hill Book Company, Inc. 1943.

7.3   Benedict, Miles, Roth, and Smity, Carnegie Inst. Pub., No. 280 (1919).

7.4   J. Nutrition, 3, 177 (1930-31).

7.5   Encyclopaedia Britannica, 1951, Volume 19, page 55.

7.6   Voit, Z. Biol., 41, 120 (1901).

7.7   Rubner, Energiegesetz, 1902, page 282.

7.8   DuBois Arch. Internal Med., 15, 868 (1915); ibid., 17, 863, 887 (1916).

7.9   Skand. Arch. Physiol., 31, 198 (1914).

7.10   Todd, J. C., Sanford, A. H., and Wells, B. B., Clinical Diagnosis by Laboratory Methods, W. B. Sunders Co., 1953.

7.11   J. Clin. Investigation 13, 615 (1934): J. D. Hardy and C. Muschenheim, ibid., 13, 817 (1934).

7.12   Burns, D., An Introduction to Biophysics, London, 1921, Chapter XXXI.

7.13   Research Bulletin 244, Univ., Mo. Agr. Expt. Stat.; see also S. Brady, Ann, Rev. Biochem., 3, 295 (1934).

APENDIX A

SYMBOLS AND CONSTANTS

The frequently used and important symbols, and the constants utilized in this book are listed below for ready reference.

A . . . . . area
B . . . . proportionality constant
C . . . . heat capacity of a substance
C_c . . . . . heat capacity due to electronic energy
C_t . . . . . heat capacity due to translational energy
C_v . . . . heat capacity due to vibrational energy
C_r . . . . heat capacity due to rotational energy
e . . . . . . energy
e_a . . . . . energy accepted by a substance
e_d . . . . . directed energy (amount of energy a substance can direct)
e_{de} . . . . . directed environmental energy
e_{dd} . . . . directed dynamic energy which flows through a substance
e_{di} . . . . . ith form of directed energy
e_{ds} . . . . . directed substance energy
e_{dw} . . . . directed exchange energy
e_e . . . . . energy of the environment at time t
e_{e0} . . . . . environmental energy at $t=0$
e_{ek} . . . . . environmental mechanical energy
e_{eT} . . . . environmental thermal energy
e_{ez} . . . . radiant energy in the environment
e_f . . . . . energy of formation

227

e_F . . . . . energy liberated by the catabolic process

e_i . . . . . energy input

e_0 . . . . . organizational energy

e_r . . . . . rejected energy

e_s . . . . . energy of a substance at time t

e_{sc} . . . . . chemical energy of a substance

e_{se} . . . . . electronic energy of a substance

e_{se0} . . . . zero state electronic energy

e_{sh} . . . . rotational energy of the molecules of a substance

e_{si} . . . . . the ith energy term of a substance

e_{sj} . . . . . energy of a substance in a given energy form j

e_{sk} . . . . . the mechanical energy of a substance

e_{sm} . . . . the mass energy of a substance

e_{s0} . . . . . energy in a substance when a closed energy system is defined

e_{st} . . . . translational energy of a substance

e_{sv} . . . . vibrational energy of a substance

e_t . . . . total energy of a system

e_w . . . . energy released to the environment by a substance

$\dot{e}_{wh}$ . . . . rate of flow of heat energy into the environment

$\dot{e}_{wm}$ . . . . rate of flow of mass energy to the environment from a substance

$\dot{e}_{ww}$ . . . . rate at which a substance performs work on the environment

e_x . . . . . semipermanent energy in a substance

e_y . . . . . transient energy in a substance

e_z . . . . . radiant energy

$\dot{e}_{\alpha}$ . . . . . rate at which environmental energy is directed toward a substance with no expendature of energy by the substance

$\dot{e}_{\alpha a}$ . . . . part of $\dot{e}_{\alpha}$ which is accepted by a substance

$\dot{e}_{\alpha r}$ . . . . part of $\dot{e}_{\alpha}$ which is rejected by a substance

$\dot{e}_{\beta}$ . . . . . rate at which environmental energy is directed toward a substance as a result of action by the substance

E . . . . . potential energy of a molecule

E_a . . . . energy level at which a molecule dissociates

E_0 . . . . ground state potential energy of a molecule

F( ) . . . a function

F . . . . . efficiency of extracting energy from food

g . . . . . thermal gradient

H . . . . . transfer function of a substance

I . . . . . . moment of inertia

k . . . . . amount of knowledge of a substance

k_e . . . . . knowledge a substance has about its environment

k_i . . . . . the ith knowledge term

k_s . . . . knowledge a substance has about itself

K . . . . . thermal conductivity of a material

L . . . . . latent heat

m . . . . . mass

m_{Fs} . . . mass of stored foodstuff in an organism

m_p . . . . mass resulting from the catabolic process

m_0 . . . . . mass of the basic structure of an organism at a particular time

M_j . . . . miscellaneous energy of a substance

Q . . . . . quantity of heat

r_0 . . . . . distance between atoms of a diatomic molecule at the point of maximum attraction

S . . . . . constant of proportionality in the knowledge equation

t . . . . . . time

t_0 . . . . . time zero i. e., the time the energy system is considered to be closed

T . . . . . temperature

Y_0 . . . . . intercept of a line with the y axis of a cartesian coordinate system

$\dot{\alpha}$ . . . . . . rate of flow of environmental energy directed toward a substance

$\dot{\beta}$ . . . . . catabolism rate in molecules of food per second

γ_h . . . . . heat energy released to the environment due to catabolism

γ_t . . . . . fractional part of energy freed in metabolism which is transferred to the environment

γ_w . . . . . work energy released to the environment due to catabolism

Δ . . . . . increment of a parameter

ϵ_s . . . . . energy of other substances in the environment

λ . . . . . the transfer function of the environment

ν . . . . . . vibrational frequency of a molecule

ν_0 . . . . . the fundamental vibrational frequency of a molecule

θ . . . . . . functional representation of the anabolism process of a plant

ω . . . . . angular velocity

∇^2 . . . . Laplace operator

$c =$ velocity of light $= 3 \times 10^{10}$ cm/sec $= 1.86 \times 10^5$ miles/sec

$h =$ Planck's constant $= 6.624 \times 10^{-27}$ erg sec

$N =$ Avogradro's number $= 6.023 \times 10^{23}$ molecules per gram-mole

$\sigma =$ Stefan-Boltzmann constant $= 5.672 \times 10^{-5}$ erg cm^{-2} deg^{-4} sec^{-1}

INDEX

A

Absolute knowledge limit, 57
Absolute temperature, 39
Adaptation, 6, 7, 154, 220
Aggregates, 41, 66
Animal knowledge, 167-215
  multi-cellular, 168
  cold blooded, 169, 175, 181
  single cell, 168
  warm blooded, 169, 175, 181
Assimilation, 113
  animals, 168
  plants, 120
Atomic energy, 15, 174
Attributes, 11
  basic knowledge, 46
Avery, 139
Avogadro's number, 99
Axiom
  knowledge, 13
  knowledge limit, 17, 18

B

Bacteria, 8, 140
Becker, 201
Benedict, 176, 178
Berkeley, 2
Biology, 16, 116
Blackman, 161
Bohr, Niels, 3
Boltzmann, 50
Botany, 16, 116
Brillouin, 52
Brody, 203
Burns, 203, 208

C

Capillary action, 119
Carbohydrates, 36, 121, 144

Catabolism, 123, 124, 151
Characteristics
  essential, mineral, 96
Clan, 204
Classes, 116
Classification
  animals, 170
  plants, 115
  system, 68, 70
Communication
  of knowledge, 49
  system, 213
Conduction, 78, 125
Conservation, law, 27, 28, 33
Convection, 79
Cook, 158
Correns, 139
Crick, 139
Crystals, 66

D

Delbrück, 139
Descartes, 2
Desoxyribonucleic acid (DNA),
  139
DeVries, 139
Diatomic molecule, 38
Diet, 203
Dissociate, 40, 90
Dissociation energy of,
    hydrogen, 97
DuBois, 201

E

Efficiency, 203
Einstein, 30, 38
Emissive power, 78
Empiricists, 2
Energy
  accepted, 33

Thermal environment, 175
Thermodynamic system, 50
Tools, 204, 211-213
Training, 203
Transfer function, mineral, 80-85
Transpiration, 119, 158
Tree knowledge, 154-165
Tribe, 204
Tschermak, 139

U

Uncertainty principle, 3
Unit, knowledge, 55-57, 218
Utility of knowledge theory, 220

V

Vital element, 114, 118
Voit, 201

W

Watson, 139
Wave mechanics, 38
White, 158
Work, 42, 45, 52, 184, 187, 193, 203